High Level Digital Marketing Strategy For Small Business Owners And Entrepreneurs

How To Market Your Business Online Without Wasting Time & Money

Nathan Williams

Copyright

Disclaimers

Limit of Liability / Disclaimer of Warranty

While the publisher and author have used their best efforts in preparing this book, they make no representations or warranties regarding the accuracy or completeness of the contents of this book. The publisher and author specifically disclaim any implied warranties of merchantability or fitness for a particular purpose, and make no guarantees whatsoever that you will achieve any particular result. Any case studies that are presented herein do not necessarily represent what you should expect to achieve, since business success depends on a variety of factors. We believe all case studies and results presented herein are true and accurate, but we have not audited the results. The advice and strategies contained in the book may not even be suitable for your situation, and you should consult your own advisors as appropriate. The publisher and author shall not be held liable for any loss of profit or any other commercial damages, including but not limited to special, incidental, consequential, or other damages. The fact that an organization or website is referred to in this work as a citation and/or a potential source of information does not mean that the publisher or author endorses the information the organization or website may provide or the recommendations it may make. Further, readers should be aware that Internet websites listed in this work may have changed or disappeared after this work was written.

Earnings Disclaimer

We don't believe in get rich programs – all human progress and accomplishment takes hard work. As stipulated by law, we cannot and do not make any guarantees about your ability to get results or earn any money with your ideas, information, tools, or strategies. After all, it takes hard work to succeed in any type of business. Nothing in this book or any of our websites is a promise or guarantee of results or future earnings, and we do not offer any legal, medical, tax, or other professional advice. Any financial numbers referenced here, or on any of our sites, are simply estimates or projections, and should not be considered exact, actual, or as a promise of potential earnings – all numbers are illustrative only.

Table Of Contents

Intro

Digital marketing can be a trip!

There are a bajillion tools and a gazillion gurus spouting their wisdom on how to do it best.

There's so much information coming at you, it's hard to know where to focus.

Here's the deal, I'm not a guru and I don't believe in using a bajillion tools ...

But, I've been using digital marketing to sell my products *(both physical and digital)*, services, and coaching for the last 4+ years ...

This book will show you how I think about digital marketing while teaching you the strategy and tactics so you can be successful as well!

MINDSET: "I Am A Direct Response Marketer"

Before getting into all the strategic and tactical stuff, we need to get on the same page with regard to **mindset**.

If you don't have the same mindset as me, you might as well stop reading ... because, you're not going to "get it".

Mindset is important because it pre-frames how you're going to use digital marketing to grow your business.

You need to have the mindset that <u>you are a direct response marketer</u>.

Every action you perform needs to focus on eliciting a specific, measured response from your visitor/customer/client/etc.

Everything you do needs to have a clear Call To Action (CTA).

For example, when you launch an ad, it needs to have a specific, measurable purpose, ie. to get email subscribers or to sell product X.

You do **NOT** launch an ad to "build awareness". WTF is "awareness"? You made people "aware" of what? Your business? What does that mean? Did they buy something? Did they become a lead? Pointless.

Another example, when you produce a piece of content, whether it's a blog post, video, podcast, etc, it needs to have a specific and measurable purpose. Who are you trying to attract? What action are you trying to get them to take? When you present your call to action (CTA), make sure you use a tracking link so you can measure your results.

Until you have money flowing out of every orifice or loads of time, every bit of marketing/advertising you do needs to have a **specific and measurable goal** - ie. leads & sales.

All that "awareness" and "branding" stuff will come over time as you grow your business ... but, when you're a startup or a small business, these are very vague goals and will lead to meager results. You need to make everything you do count.

Does that make sense?

I hope so, and I hope we are in agreement because, if not ... save yourself some time and stop reading now.

Lay Your Groundwork

Before moving on to marketing, you need to have your business fundamentals down first.

Customers

You need to know who your customers are, their pain points, where they congregate online, etc.

If you don't know who you're trying to reach, it's going to be mighty hard to market to them.

If you don't know who your customers are, please watch this video here: https://crazyeyemarketing.com/dms/customers

Business

Obviously, you need a business with products and/or services before you can market it. But there's a good chance you haven't put much thought into the "structure" of what you have to offer.

You need to think about how your offerings provide value to your customers.

What are your up-sells, down-sells, and cross-sells?

How do you "ascend" your customers to give them more value while your business generates more money?

If you just kinda "sell some stuff" and there's no real rhyme, reason, or flow between what you sell ...

I highly recommend you focus on establishing your value ladder (ANNEX A) before moving on.

Even if your offerings are structured in a way to "ascend" people, I still recommend checking out the ANNEX on Value Ladders as it will serve as a good refresher.

Delivery

The final piece of groundwork you need in place before moving on is a way to deliver your offerings.

Maybe you have a brick & mortar business, or an ecommerce store, or maybe you have a membership portal ... whatever the way, it doesn't matter.

The point is, you need to have a way to collect money and deliver the goods.

And, 9 times out of 10 ... the way you currently collect money and deliver your offerings is sub par, but it's OK. We're going to optimize the heck out of it when we get to the Point Of Sale Optimization segment!

The Sales Funnel Concept

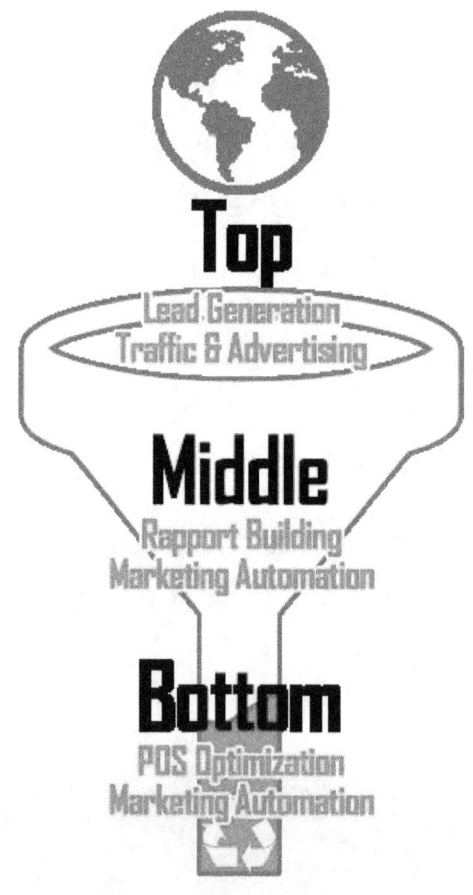

Moving forward, you need to think of your digital marketing efforts like a funnel ...

There's a big world out there with over 7 billion people on it.

Some of them need what you have, but most people don't.

We call the people that need what you offer your ideal customer, marketing persona, or avatar.

You attract this individual through advertising.

There are many ways to advertise and we'll get into them in another part, but all advertising needs to have the specific and measurable goal of acquiring leads.

When you have leads, you're able to use marketing automation to develop a relationship with them and build rapport.

These relationships help you convert leads into paying customers.

And, when you have a paying customer, you want to make sure you're offering them as much value as possible for days/weeks/months/years to come.

Fortunately, much of this can also be accomplished with the help of marketing automation.

And that, my friend, is the sales funnel concept.

Of course, there are a lot of moving parts inside of it *(we'll be getting to them)*, but that's the big picture.

Moving On!

If you've made it this far, it's because you have taken on the mindset of a direct response marketer, have your business fundamentals in place, and have a general understanding of the sales funnel concept.

Now, it's time to get into the nitty-gritty digital marketing strategy and tactics!

(part 1) How To Drive High Quality Traffic To Your Business

Traffic. The lifeblood of your digital marketing efforts. Without it - you have nothing.

There are a million ways to generate traffic and every minute someone is coming out with a new, "best" way to do it.

Here's the deal, you only need to focus on two sources of traffic:

1. **One** organic "free" source
2. **One** paid source

Before we get into which sources you should use and why, we need to talk about the #1 rule of traffic.

The #1 Rule Of Traffic

As I said earlier, there are a million ways to generate traffic ... so, there are a lot of shiny objects, a lot of people pushing which traffic generation method is "best".

It can be very tempting to get sucked into whatever they're offering ... and, you know what, usually, what they're offering isn't half bad EXCEPT

1. It takes you away from what you need to focus on
2. It likely breaks the #1 rule of traffic

So, what is the #1 rule?

You need to be where your customers are.

Duh.

But, this rule gets broken all the time because someone creates this juicy concept/tool and you grab it because it promises easy traffic.

Next thing you know, you're posting 50 times a day on Pinterest trying to attract 30-year-old males. *(there are very few 30-year-old males on Pinterest ... and yes, that's from a past experience ...)*

Or, you launched a Snapchat profile and story aimed at attracting 60-year-old women. *(there are few 60-year-olds on Snapchat)*

So, do yourself a favor ... the next time you're getting persuaded to buy some fancy new tool to drive traffic, I urge you not to buy it until you read this full section. At the very least, make sure it will actually reach your audience.

Organic "Free" Traffic

Moving forward, you will have **ONE** source for organic traffic and **ONE** source for paid traffic. *(More on paid traffic in the next section)*

So, what is organic traffic? Organic traffic is the traffic that naturally finds your content and your business.

Some people call organic traffic, "free" traffic, because it doesn't cost money; however, **it *certainly* costs time**.

Here are a few organic traffic sources so you understand what I mean:

- Search Engine Optimization (SEO) - blogging
- Social Media - Facebook, Twitter, Instagram, LinkedIn, Pinterest, Snapchat, Musical.ly
- Video - YouTube
- Podcasts - iTunes, Stitcher, SoundCloud

Here's The 411...

If you read the intro, you may recall that I gave "awareness" and "branding" a hard time because it's neither specific nor measurable.

Ok, for the most part, the results from your organic traffic efforts will be hard to quantify accurately.

You can track as much as possible by using site tracking tools like Google Analytics and link tracking tools like bit.ly and Pretty Link, but - at the end of the day, you're at the mercy of the environment you choose to operate in.

My point is, since it's hard to accurately measure your efforts already, organic traffic is the place to grow "awareness" and "branding"!

This is your chance to be your weird, funky self and show people *who* you and your business are!

* Note: just because organic traffic can be hard to track and you get to be your weird, funky self – it doesn't mean you should create content willy-nilly. Everything you create still needs to serve a purpose and be as specific and measurable as possible.

The Organic Traffic Strategy

This is important.

Only pick _ONE_ organic traffic source to focus _100%_ of your efforts.

That's right, if you choose Instagram ... that's ALL you're going to focus on. Yes, I know, it seems "logical" to do Facebook, Twitter, Tumblr, and Flickr too since you can post to all those networks at the same time you post to Instagram ... and by having more content in more places you "should" reach more eyes ... right? **WRONG!**

Each platform has its own set of "rules" whether by design or via social norms.

By "bulk" posting, you will spread yourself too thin and possibly alienate different platforms ... which, you don't want to do.

Instead, you focus only on **_ONE_ source**. **100%** of your focus is on growing that channel **until you have a significant following**.

The size of a "significant following" will vary tremendously based on a number of variables like market size. For example, if you're a brick & mortar business and there are 2,000 ideal customers in a 25-mile radius from your store and 1,500 of them follow you on Instagram ... you're doing pretty freakin' good!

You also need to take into account **engagement**. Who cares if you have 10k followers on Instagram if you only get 100 likes/comments when you post? The "real" size of your following is much closer to 100 than that inflated 10k number.

Once you have a significant following on **ONE** source *THEN* you open the next source and "feed" it with the following you built on your original source.

A good percentage of people will make the jump because most people are on multiple platforms and they can follow you elsewhere with a click or tap.

So, that's how you do it. Focus 100% of your efforts on **ONE** source. Take courses on how to become "good" at that source. Get yourself some fancy tools if you want. Do whatever it takes to really grow that ONE source. Once the first one is rockin' & rollin', add another source and jump start it by sending your audience over to it.

How Do You Pick Your _ONE_ Source?

How you pick your ONE source is pretty simple...

- It must follow the #1 rule - you need to be where your customers are

- It must be something you like doing

That's it!

If you like writing and your audience likes reading ... start a blog.

If you like taking photos and sharing inspirational quotes and your audience likes looking at photos and quotes ... start an Instagram profile.

If you like talking and your audience likes to listen ... start a podcast.

My one piece of advice is this, NEVER do something you don't like doing because you won't stick with it.

For example, I've tried a dozen times to focus on growing my Facebook following because I know my audience is there and it's a good place to generate traffic. However, after 3 days I quit because ... you know what ... I'm an introvert and being "social" is something I'm just not comfortable with or naturally good at doing.

However, I enjoy writing and blogging. As such, I have a blog and attract visitors through Google and other search engines.

Paid Traffic

It's been said, *"You don't have a business until you can convert paid traffic."*

Here's the deal - **you don't control *organic* traffic.**

Let me say it again - **YOU DON'T CONTROL *ORGANIC* TRAFFIC!**

Platforms change. Algorithms change. Markets change.

With organic traffic, you're at the mercy of the platform you've chosen to pursue.

For example, 90% of our business on Crazy Eye Marketing comes from Google and YouTube.

If Google decides to drop Crazy Eye Marketing in the search results ... our business could vanish ... except, we know how to send paid traffic!

Once you're able to take $1, put it into an advertising campaign and get that $1 *and more* back ... **you're unstoppable.**

Paid traffic also makes it very easy to define specific goals and measure the results.

So, why do I keep it at 90% organic and 10% paid? Because it's working and organic traffic is "free" ... my customer acquisition costs are essentially zero beyond the time I spend developing content, which is, at this point, a sunk cost.

But, if Google decides to drop the hammer, we'll flip on our paid campaigns and keep trucking right along!

My point is, **you need to know how to pay for traffic.**

Before You Start Spending Money!

If you've ever "tried" paid advertising before and been astonished by how much it can cost to get someone to click your ad and wondered how it could possibly be viable ... it's because you didn't have a Micro Sales Funnel in place.

Before you spend a dime on paid advertising, you need to have a Micro Sales Funnel setup and ready to go.

While I'm going to cover Micro Sales Funnels in detail in part 6, the simple definition of a Micro Sales Funnel is **a system specifically designed to acquire leads and rapidly convert them into customers.**

For example, Nathan is surfing Facebook when he sees an ad for the Top 10 Facebook Ads of 2016. Nathan clicks the ad and lands on a page that requests his name and email (a squeeze page) in exchange for the top 10 ads. Immediately after entering his contact info, he's greeted with an offer to get the top 15 WORST Facebook Ads of 2016 for only $7. Nathan thinks, "Shoot, I don't want to make the same mistakes as them, let me grab that!" and he spends $7. Immediately after purchasing the 15 worst ads, he's made an offer to join a course on Facebook Ad Optimization so he can create great ads for only $97. Nathan grabs it. Immediately afterwards, he's presented yet another offer for a training course on creating high converting sales pages for $297. He turns it down because he's a marketing genius and doesn't need help building landing pages.

All told, Nathan spends $104. Some people spend $0. And others spend $401.

All of a sudden, the average order size per click is $3. So, if the business can spend less than $3 per click, they're essentially printing money!

That's how paid advertising works.

You absolutely, positively, need a way to make your money back ASAP!

Of course, there's the whole long game where your customers' lifetime value should increase over time ... but, **the goal is an immediate return on your investment.**

If you can lock that down, you'll be unstoppable!

Paid Traffic Fundamentals

As with organic traffic, you're only going to focus on _**ONE**_ source of paid traffic.

For the sake of moving forward and making progress, there are only two paid traffic sources you should consider:

1. Facebook Ads Manager

2. Google Adwords

That's it. At least a fraction of your customers are on Facebook and/or using Google.

If your audience is not on either of those platforms ... they're not online and you shouldn't be focusing on digital marketing.

So, pick one or the other and let's move on!

After making your decision, you need to immerse yourself in the platform. Take courses, listen to podcasts, read blog posts and articles ... become a beast on that particular platform.

What You Need To Pay Attention To

While you're immersing yourself in the ad platform of your choosing, there are a few key elements you really need to pay attention to.

These elements are often overlooked by small business owners and entrepreneurs when they launch paid advertising campaigns.

I really want to emphasize their importance here because they're the difference between success and failure.

Also note, the two aforementioned advertising platforms **want you to be successful**. Because, if you're successful, you'll keep spending money ... so, they give you a lot of tools to help you out.

The key elements you need to know about and implement are:

- **Micro Sales Funnels** - Already mentioned a bunch of times, so DO IT or you're going to fail or, at the very least, have meager results. [see part 6]

- **Conversion Tracking** - There are pieces of code called "pixels" that you will need to place on your website that communicate with the advertising platform and can signal when conversions (ie. leads and sales) take place. You need this so you know what is/isn't working and it helps the advertising platform auto-optimize your campaigns for better results.

- **Audiences** - Both platforms allow you to create audiences in a variety of ways. Everything from being able to upload customer email addresses, your email lists' email addresses, website visitors, lookalike audiences, custom audiences, smart audiences, and beyond. You need to understand the various audience types and how you can take advantage of them because they can make or break your campaigns.

Summary

That's traffic generation in a nutshell.

The key things to remember are ...

- Focus on **_ONE_** source of organic traffic and
- **_ONE_** source of paid traffic

Once you nail the one source of each down, you can branch out by using the audience and systems you've built with your first sources.

(part 2) How To Capture More Leads The Right Way

In part 1 we discussed mastering two sources for traffic: 1 organic "free" source and 1 paid source.

In part 2 here, we're going to discuss what to *actually* do with the traffic once you have it ... you're going to start building your list<u>S</u>!

There's <u>MORE</u> Than 1 List!

You've likely heard the saying, "The money is in the list."

99% of the time, the "list" people are referring to is an *email* list. And, this section is primarily about email lists, however...

I'm going to let you in on a little secret ... **there are more list types than *just* email.**

Of course, there's physical address lists for things like direct mail and phone lists so you can call your leads and customers.

But, there are also **audience lists**. *(sometimes called retargeting or remarketing lists)*

Audience lists are built within advertising platforms, ie. Facebook's Ad Manager and Google Adwords.

Individuals are added to your audience lists when they perform a particular action, such as, visit your site, view specific pages, purchase a product or service, watch a video, among other reasons.

You're then able to place ads in front of individuals on your audience lists, which keeps them in your funnel and aware of your business.

My point is, before you read the rest of this chapter, *which mainly concerns email lists*, I want you to realize and understand there are other list types out there because it's going to open a whole world of opportunity for you.

Also, in part 4 we're going to go into more detail on advertising to *(or retargeting)* these audience lists.

Let's Talk About Your Email List

Having a list of email addresses is important.

It's an asset.

It grants you the power to reach out and communicate with your audience.

It's permission based marketing.

This means people have given you permission to contact them.

They've *asked* you to send them emails.

You're not "annoying" people with ads as they browse Facebook or the web, trying to get them to buy your stuff.

They *want* to hear from you.

At least, this is the goal. Of course, you can treat a list poorly, burn bridges, harass people, etc., but, you're not going to do that because you're a good person and a responsible business owner!

You can change its medium.

You can do more with a list of email addresses than just send emails to it...

You can upload it into advertising platforms like Facebook and Google Adwords to create audience lists.

Yes! Let's say you have a list of 10,000 email addresses, you can upload that list straight into Facebook and they'll automatically pair those email addresses with the associated profiles, giving you the power to target people on your email list! *(insanely powerful!)*

You control it.

Unlike the "audience lists" I mentioned above that *technically* belong to whatever advertising platform you built them on - ie. Facebook Ads Manager or Google Adwords ... an email list is <u>*yours*</u>.

You can move it from one marketing automation tool to the next.

You can manually send emails.

You can upload it into the audience list tools to build custom audiences.

You can do a lot with an email list.

Having a <u>**QUALITY**</u> email list is one of the keys to success in digital marketing.

Quality? Yes, although it should go without saying ... the size of the list isn't as important as who's actually on it.

If you have a list of 100,000 people, but they all live in India or Pakistan and you're trying to get them to visit your ecommerce store that only ships products in the US ... those 100,000 people aren't worth a dime.

Whereas, if you have 10,000 raving fans on your list and every time you send an email with an offer, a good percent jumps on it (~5%) ... you're golden. Unstoppable!

Ok, So How Do You Grow An Email List?

Side note: There are businesses and individuals that will sell you lists of email addresses. Depending on where you live, this is illegal and at the very least, unethical. Remember the permission based marketing remarks above? Yeah, you're definitely violating that relationship if you buy a random list from someone.

There are many different strategies, tactics, tricks, hacks, etc. for growing your email list ... but, they all follow one core principle: **Give an individual something of value in exchange for their contact information.**

In the digital marketing world, the "something" you give to an individual is called a "Lead Magnet".

A few example Lead Magnets are:

- Coupons/Discounts
- Checklists
- eBooks
- Contest/Raffle Entry
- Free Trial
- Course Access
- Webinars
- Flowcharts/Frameworks
- Mind Maps

You've likely seen most of these offered in one form or another as you've browsed the Internet.

It's a pretty simple concept, but it works across all niches and markets.

There's more information on Lead Magnets in ANNEX B.

Growing Your Email List With Traffic You _DON'T_ Control

As long as you have a website with something of value on it and you do a little bit of promotion through your organic "free" traffic source ... people will eventually visit it.

Sometimes, you can control what page they're going to land on. If you've grown your Facebook page audience and you post a link to a blog post ... you're pre-framing that traffic and controlling where they land.

In other instances, you won't have any control over what page someone visits. Like, if someone finds your site through a Google search ... you can't control what page they're going to land on. They're going to land wherever they're going to land!

My point is, people are going to find your stuff in some of the most random of ways and **you need to be prepared** to capture their contact information.

The best way to grow your email list with traffic you don't control is with opt-in forms.

Grow Your Email List With Opt-in Forms

There are many types and triggers for opt-in forms; however, for the sake of an example - an opt-in form is a form that pops-up when an individual lands on a website that asks for their contact information in exchange for a Lead Magnet.

Opt-in forms provide the benefit of being able to placed *anywhere* on your site; ie. if a visitor lands on a random blog post, you can present an opt-in form.

For example:

Most people have a love/hate relationship with opt-in forms.

As a visitor to a website, they can be incredibly annoying ... especially when they keep popping over what you're trying to read.

But, as the site owner, we know those pop-up opt-in forms tend to work. So, we keep showing them.

This creates an interesting dichotomy, but that's beyond the scope of this particular section.

The point is, **they work** and you should use them to capture traffic you don't control.

For more information on opt-in forms and tools to use, check out ANNEX C.

Growing Your Email List With Traffic You _DO_ Control

There are many instances when you control where your audience lands, ie. you're paying for it, you send a link in an email, you post a link on your social media profile, etc.

In this section, I'm mainly referring to the **traffic you're paying for.**

If you're paying for people to visit your site, you better have a plan!

I've seen far too many small business owners sending paid traffic to their homepage to "raise awareness" ... which, as you know, isn't specific or measurable and therefore, wasted effort.

When you're spending money on traffic, think of it like fishing.

You're fishing in Facebook's/Google's lake for your ideal prospects. What bait (Lead Magnet) are you going to use to draw them in? How are you going to catch them so you can place them in your lake (ie. your email list)?

#1 Goal, Grow Your Email List

Make the #1 goal of your paid advertising campaigns **growing your email list**!

* Side note: There are other reasons why you will pay for traffic. For example, when we discuss retargeting in part 4 you will pay to attract those that are already on your list; however, for all intents and purposes, your #1 goal for paid traffic is to grow that email list!

One of the best ways to grow your email list with paid traffic is to send people directly to a landing page, sometimes called a squeeze page because it "squeezes" the contact information out of the individual.

Simply put, it's one page with one objective/goal, offer a Lead Magnet in exchange for contact info. That's it.

Here's an example:

And another:

SAVE 50%: Monkey Fist – Self Defense Keychain

STEP 1: Enter Your Contact Information Below

| Your Name |
| Your Email |

CONTINUE TO STEP 2

Simple enough, right?

It's not complicated.

Create an ad that says, "Want this super awesome [Lead Magnet]? Click here!", which takes them to a squeeze page asking for name, email, etc. so you can send [Lead Magnet] right over.

The individual opts-in for your Lead Magnet and now they're on your email list!

Don't forget, make sure you're tracking conversions and using pixels PROPERLY when sending paid traffic to your squeeze pages!

Note: These squeeze pages are typically the first step in a Micro Sales Funnel (part 6)

In Closing...

You need to grow your list**S**!

You need to grow your audience lists within the advertising platforms (ie. Facebook and Google Adwords) by using conversion tracking and pixels.

And, more importantly, you need to grow your email list because **you own it**.

The best way to grow your email list is by offering a Lead Magnet in exchange for contact information. The best way to offer your Lead Magnets depends upon where the traffic is coming from:

- For organic "free" traffic, use different types of opt-in forms

- For paid traffic, use squeeze pages

Remember, this is not meant to be overly complicated. It's a simple process that you can see examples of everywhere.

It's just a matter of doing it and growing your various list**S**!

(part 3) How To Use Marketing Automation To Generate Sales

I *love* the era we live in.

The technology that's available can save us so much time by helping us automate portions of our business.

For example, you can automate emails, text messages, direct mail, and ringless voicemails.

Not to mention the fact you can automate your entire social media presence or outsource tasks to virtual assistants, freeing you to focus on "bigger" things.

There's so much opportunity to automate portions of your business, that if you're not ... you're not only wasting time and money, but **you're missing out on growth.**

This section is all about using marketing automation to help generate sales.

Transactional Communication

Transactional communications (email/text/direct mail/ringless voicemail) are the easiest and most logical communications to implement and automate.

If someone requests a Lead Magnet, you send them what they requested.

If someone purchases a product or service, you send them a receipt and/or more information.

If someone abandons their cart, you remind them about it.

This makes sense, right? Nothing revolutionary here.

But, you still gotta do it. The money is made by following the basics.

#1 Goal Of Transactional Communication

The #1 goal of transactional communication is to **present your next offer.** *(now is a great time to ensure you have a Value Ladder! [ANNEX A])*

Examples:

- An individual requests a Lead Magnet, you present the product/service that complements the Lead Magnet

- An individual purchases a product or service, you present complementary products/services

- An individual abandons their cart, you remind them about the products in their cart and possibly include a discount or bonus to drive them back to complete the checkout process

Again, this is no-brainer stuff right here, but it's overlooked so often I have to bring it up.

Relationship Building

In part 2 we discussed capturing people's contact information so you can follow up with them later.

Beyond sending transactional communications, you can send more "generalized" communications that build and maintain relationships, promote your products and services, and gauge interest *(more on that later)*.

What does it mean to send "relationship building" communications?

It means that you're sending **valuable content**. For example, blog posts, videos, audios, infographics, stories, Q&A, support, etc.

Now, just because you're sending valuable content, it doesn't mean that it can't link to your products/services sales pages or that you can't use it to "mold" your leads and customers to conform to your way of thinking!

It's kind of like propaganda without the whole "misleading" part. You will never, ever mislead people on purpose. Right? *But*, you can teach them your ways if you believe them to be better than what's out there.

Before you know it, you'll become the authority and they'll follow you anywhere. *(that's the goal at least!)*

How To Build A Relationship

Too many small business owners and entrepreneurs overthink the sending of communications.

They worry about sending too many emails and annoying their leads and customers.

Or, they're not sure what to send.

I'm telling you right here, right now ... it's not rocket science.

Talk to your audience like you normally would. Share what you would normally share.

You don't have to use fancy pants tactics and copywriting hacks to send an email.

Be a human being talking to other human beings. Really. That's it. That's the secret.

Now, there are some general rules of thumb if you're completely lost...

General Rules Of Thumb

1. **Email 3-4 times a week**. Any less and they'll forget about you. Any more and you may become a nuisance.

2. **1 promotional "sales" email every 2 weeks**. ie. share more valuable content than promotional content.

   1. Remember, that's not to say your valuable content can't have links to your promotional/sales material!

A Pattern

I know some folks are like, "I really, really, really, really need a formula or pattern to follow! Just give me the freakin' formula!!!"

Ok, check out ANNEX D for an email pattern to follow.

You Gotta Gauge Interest!

We've just talked about transactional communications, where if someone performs an action, you send them something.

And, we also talked about relationship building communications, where you're sharing valuable content in order to get people to know, like, and trust you and your business.

Now, it's time to merge the two!

Introducing the Interest Driven Sales Funnel concept!

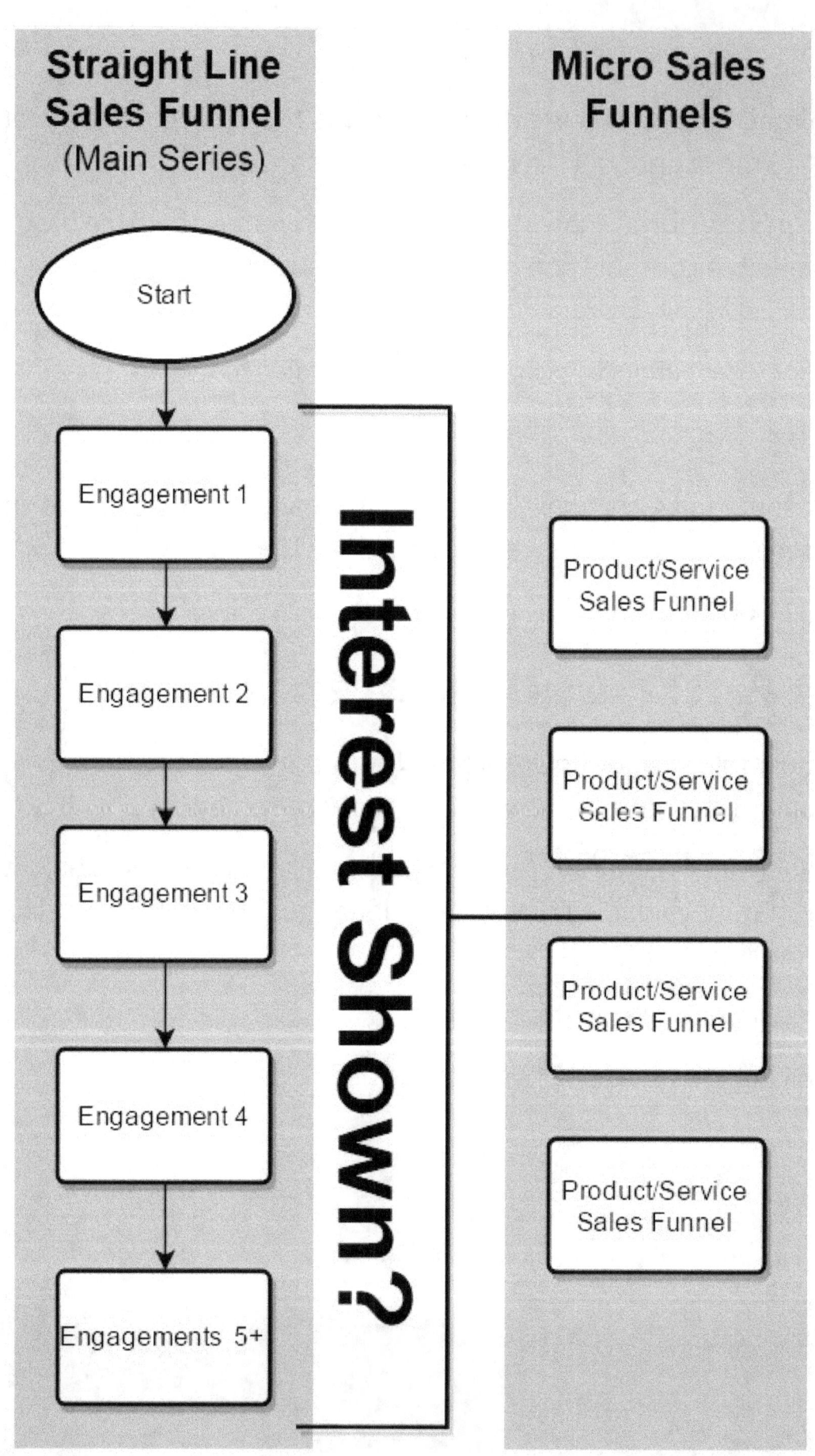

On the left hand side we have our "Straight Line Sales Funnel" or "Main Series".

The "Main Series" contains all of our relationship building communications or engagements, ie. emails, ads, etc.

When an individual engages with a piece of valuable content we send, they're automatically placed in a "Micro Sales Funnel" or "Product/Service Sales Funnel".

The "Micro Sales Funnel's" purpose is to drive the individual to take action, ie. buy something, register for something, etc. This is accomplished by sending more, relevant content to the individual in an effort to persuade them to buy a particular product/service.

A quick example: Let's pretend I run an ecommerce store that sells kitchenware. I offer three categories of products: flatware, pots & pans, and cutlery. I send out a piece of communications with a link to an article called, "The Best Way To Clean A Kitchen Knife". If an individual clicks that link, I know they're interested in kitchen knives and they're automatically entered into my Micro Sales Funnel with the sole purpose to get them to purchase my self-cleaning, state of the art, kitchen knife!

It's much easier to sell someone something when they've already shown interest in it.

Micro Sales Funnels can range in complexity from very simple, like sending a few emails on a topic the person showed interest in, to full blown funnels featuring 1-click upsells, downsells, and everything in between.

We'll be going into greater detail on Micro Sales Funnels in part 6 of this guide.

That's the Interest Driven Sales Funnel concept in a nutshell ... figure out what someone is interested in and then try to sell them a product/service based on that interest.

The Tools

In our opinion, the best marketing automation tool on the market today is ActiveCampaign.

It lets you send emails and text messages **PLUS** it connects to Zapier which connects to over 750 other apps that do anything and everything from sending direct mail, to ringless voicemails, and beyond!

ActiveCampaign allows you to create automations for transactional and relationship building communications, while helping you gauge interest(s) via tagging that can trigger Micro Sales Funnel automations.

ActiveCampaign is a very solid marketing automation tool and one we highly recommend.

Summary

You need to take advantage of marketing automation. It will save you time and money while simultaneously helping you grow your business by converting more leads into paying customers.

Marketing automation really shines when it comes to sending transactional and relationship building communications. Plus, you can merge the two concepts into an Interest Driven Sales Funnel!

Finally, there are a lot of tools on the market to help you with marketing automation; however, the best tool we've found is ActiveCampaign.

(part 4) How To Use Retargeting To Generate Sales

Have you ever looked at a product on Amazon and then seen ads for that same product on Facebook, CNN, and other unrelated sites as you browsed the web?

If so, you've experienced retargeting! *(sometimes referred to as remarketing)*

Retargeting is a powerful tool that, when combined with marketing automation, creates an unstoppable marketing force!

How Retargeting Works

Retargeting gives you the ability to **_show ads_ to people on your audience lists**.

As a reminder, these audience lists are lists of people that are built within the advertising platform you've chosen to master, ie. Facebook or Adwords.

You're able to add people to your audience lists in a variety of ways such as:

- **Website activity**: pages viewed or pages *not* viewed

- **Customer files**: upload a list of email addresses and/or other contact information and the ad platform will sync that information with users in their database, allowing you to retarget people already on your email list, customer list, phone list, etc.

- **Engagement** (applies to Facebook): how much of your video(s) they've consumed, if they've interacted with your Facebook Page, or if they've clicked on a Lead Ad or opened a Canvas

You're also able to define how long an individual will stay on your audience list before they "fall off". Ie. if you only want to target people who have visited your site in the last 7 days and didn't buy anything, you can do that. That way you're only advertising to people who recently ran across your business.

Lookalike/Similar Audiences

One of the best parts about creating an audience list is that both Facebook and Adwords allow you to create Lookalike or Similar Audiences.

What does this mean?

Say, for example, you have a list of 3,000 customers' email addresses. You can upload that list to Facebook or Adwords and they'll sync those email addresses with individuals on their platform.

Then, if you create a Lookalike/Similar Audience, the ad platform will "blend" all 3,000 of those individuals' likes, dislikes, habits, demographics, behaviors, etc. and create what is essentially a customer avatar. They'll figure out the characteristics of your average customer.

Then, they'll take that customer avatar and find a percentage of people that most closely resembles that avatar. For example, if you're on Facebook and you create a Lookalike Audience targeting 1% of the US population, you'll end up with a Lookalike Audience of roughly 2 million people that look most like your customer avatar.

Doing this helps you find people most likely to connect with your business!

Super powerful and something you need to study and understand!

Combine Marketing Automation (Email) With Retargeting

As you're aware, the effectiveness of email has declined in the last few years because it's easy to do and everyone is doing it. Since everyone is doing it, people are bombarded with emails, and they've learned to ignore the "noise" in their inbox.

This is all OK.

You still need to focus on building your email list because **it's an asset**.

When you have something you *really* want your audience to see, simply combine email marketing with retargeting.

How? I'll show you because I'm doing this exact thing right now....

Step 1: Export your list of email subscribers that you want to see your message

Step 2: Create a custom audience in your ad platform by uploading the list of email subscribers you just exported

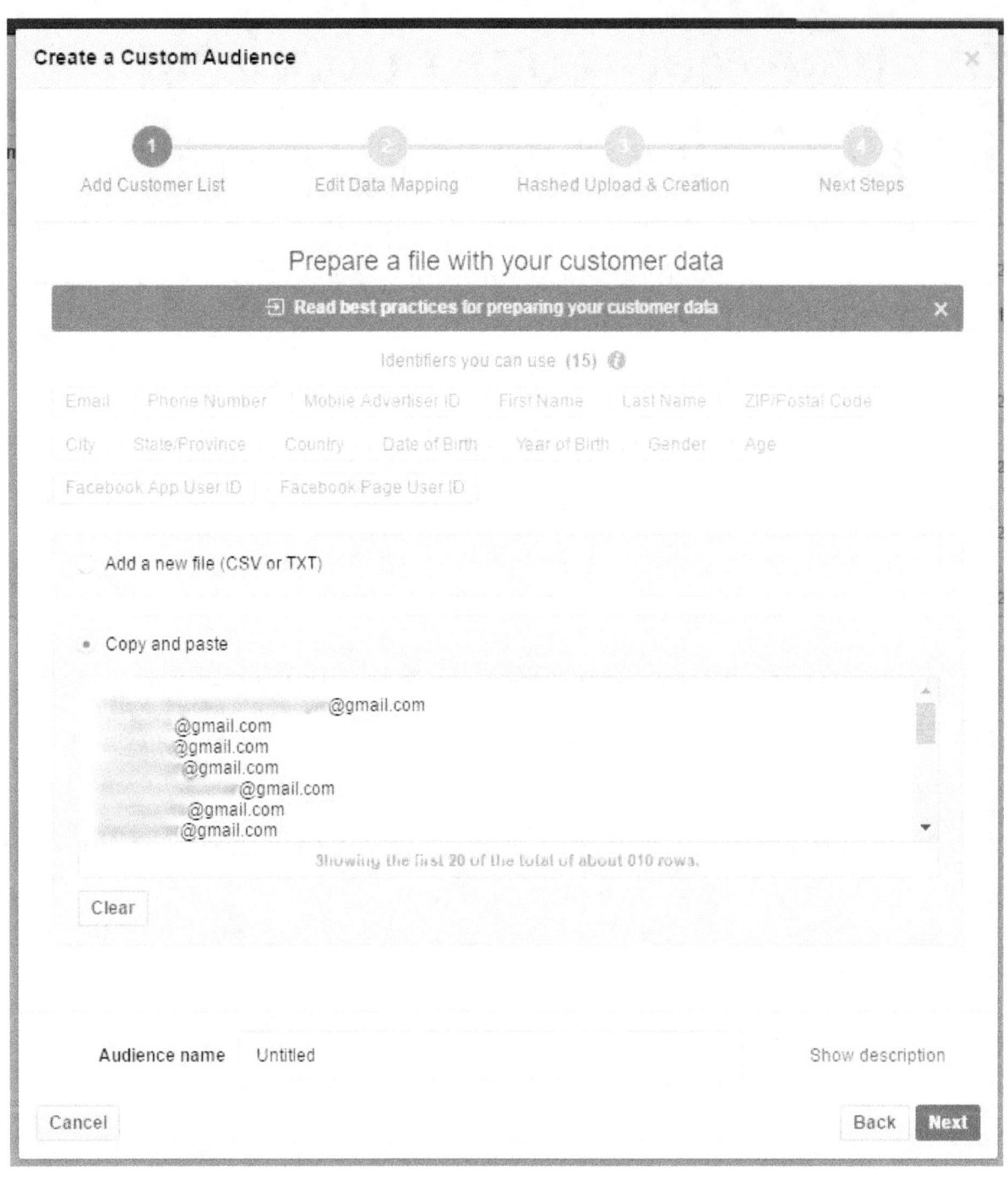

Create a Custom Audience

1 — Add Customer List
2 — Edit Data Mapping
3 — Hashed Upload & Creation
4 — Next Steps

Prepare a file with your customer data

↪ **Read best practices for preparing your customer data** ✕

Identifiers you can use (15) ℹ️

Email	Phone Number	Mobile Advertiser ID	First Name	Last Name	ZIP/Postal Code
City	State/Province	Country	Date of Birth	Year of Birth	Gender	Age
Facebook App User ID	Facebook Page User ID

○ Add a new file (CSV or TXT)

● Copy and paste

@gmail.com
@gmail.com
@gmail.com
@gmail.com
@gmail.com
@gmail.com
@gmail.com

Showing the first 20 of the total of about 010 rows.

Clear

Audience name   Untitled   Show description

Cancel   Back   **Next**

Step 3: Launch your ad targeting that audience list

Crazy Eye Marketing
2 hrs · 🌐

You're seeing this ad because you're on our email list and we want to let you know that tonight @ 10PM EST ... the price of The Sales Funnel Vault is going from $347 to $497.

If you're serious about multiplying your business with marketing automation (which I imagine you are or you wouldn't be seeing this ad) today is a great day to sign up for our training program!

Learn more: https://crazyeyemarketing.com/join/

You're on the list!

Learn how to multiply your business with marketing automation.

CRAZYEYEMARKETING.COM

Learn More

Step 4: Send your email

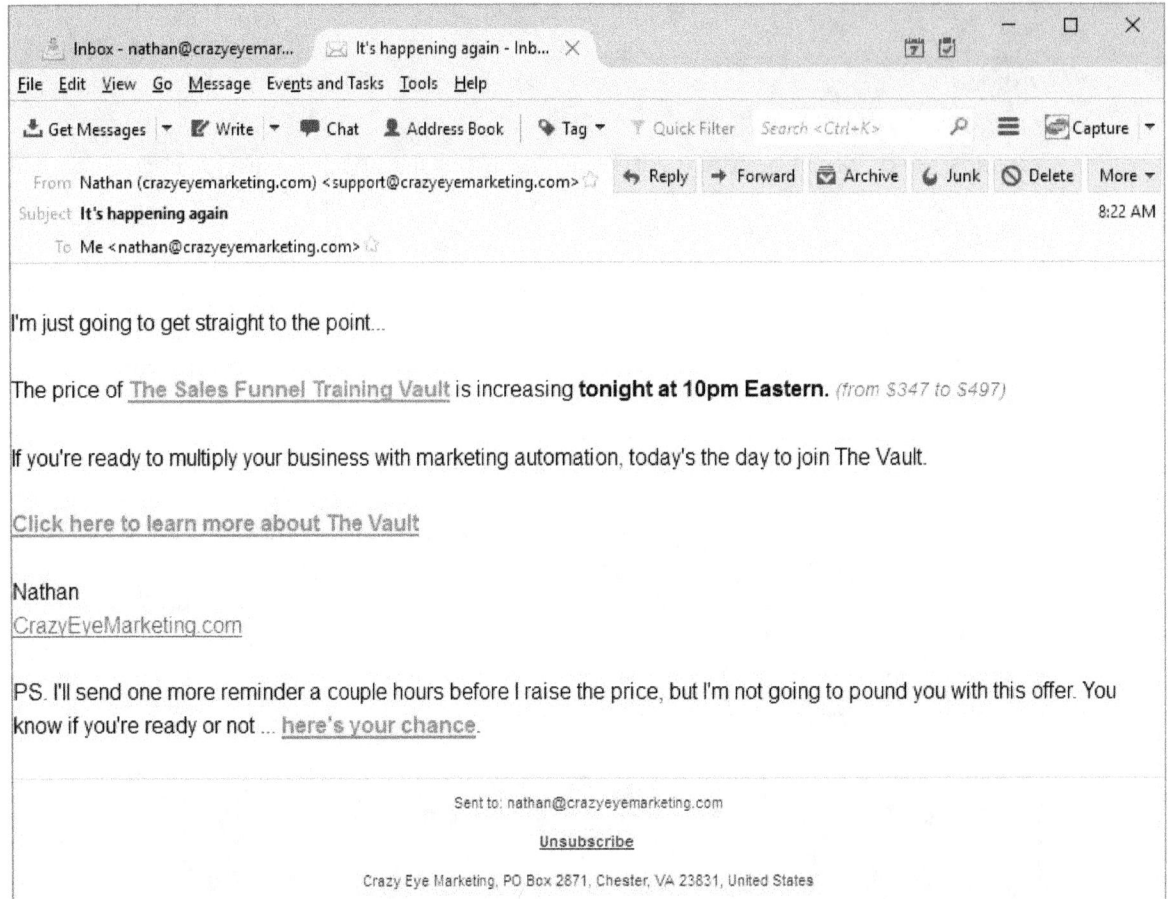

BOOM!

Now, I have my message greeting people in two separate places: their inbox and as they browse Facebook.

There's no escaping my important message.

Do you see how I'm combining the two? I hope so and I hope you see how powerful that is!

Retargeting Strategies

Thanks to the flexibility and power of audience lists and retargeting, there are a million and one different strategies you can employ.

I already let you in on one strategy, retarget your list of email subscribers with the same message you sent via email to ensure they see it, whether in their inbox or while browsing Facebook.

While I can't cover all of the many strategies here, I'll share a few popular concepts to help you "think" in the right direction.

Visited Site, But Didn't Opt-in

One of the most popular retargeting strategies is to retarget individuals that have visited your website, but didn't join your email list.

Maybe they didn't see your opt-in form or maybe they weren't interested in the Lead Magnet you offered.

Whatever the reason, they left your site without opting-in. *However,* they **did** visit your site which means they were interested in what you have to offer and they now know who you are ... so, if you show them any ads, they'll be more familiar with your business.

The strategy is to retarget these people with other Lead Magnets. Maybe they didn't like the first one you showed them. No problem, show them one on a completely different topic or one that's in a different format (ie. a coupon vs. a checklist vs. a video course).

You keep trying to bring them back until they're on your email list!

Pro-tip! Clicks & Video Views

To "boost" the number of visitors that land on your site, one strategy is to launch an ad with the goal of getting people to visit your site. For example, you write an amazing blog article that you want people in your niche to see. So, you create an ad that "boosts" that blog post in front of your ideal customers, they see the ad, read the article (visit your site), then you retarget them with ads that offer different Lead Magnets.

This works well because getting "clicks" to a website is typically cheaper than other advertising goals like conversions.

Another way you can do this is by running a video ad with the goal of "video views". Like "clicks", "video views" tend to be cheaper than the other advertising goals available which allow your ad spend to go further.

So, the strategy is to push your video ad in front of as many ideal customers as possible and retarget those that watch 50%+ of your video. Kind of like reading a blog article, if they watch more than half of your video, they've become familiar with your business and your offer; now, it's time to retarget them with Lead Magnets until they're on your email list!

Looked At Product, But Didn't Buy

This one is self-explanatory ... if someone looks at your product/service, but doesn't purchase it, retarget them with ads to bring them back to your offer.

You could also include a coupon with your retargeting ad to really incentivize them to take action!

Bought This, But Not That

Also, self-explanatory. If someone buys one product from you, but doesn't take the upsell or any of the complementary products, you retarget them with ads promoting the products they're likely interested in.

For example, if someone buys a set of kitchen knives, a complementary product would be a knife sharpener. So, a good retargeting ad would offer that person a discount on knife sharpeners.

Pull'em Through The Funnel

You're able to pull people through your sales funnel with audience lists and retargeting ads.

I'll illustrate this with an example.

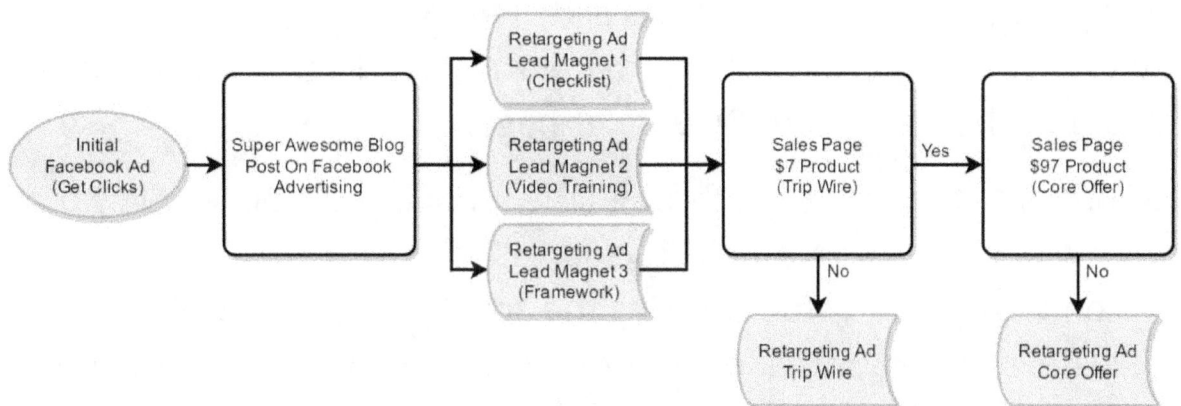

Let's say you want to sell a $97 course on Facebook Ads (Core Offer), so you setup a Micro Sales Funnel (part 6) to attract people, educate them, and ultimately sell your course.

You decided to write a "Super Awesome Blog Post On Facebook Advertising" and you're sending as much traffic to that post as possible via Facebook Ads.

Every person that lands on your article is then "pixeled" and added to an audience list you've created.

You then promote ads to that audience list with offers for 3 different Lead Magnets. They all have to do with Facebook advertising; however, one is a checklist, one is video training, and one is a framework for people to follow.

Individuals will then opt-in to your email list when they request a Lead Magnet, so you can follow up with them via email in addition to retargeting.

The first product you offer after they opt-in is a $7 product, sometimes called a Trip Wire because it's priced so low, people can't help but grab it and "trip" into your Core Offer.

If they don't buy your Trip Wire right away, retarget them with ads that bring them back to your sales page.

If they *do* buy your Trip Wire, offer them your Core Offer (the $97 Facebook Course). If they buy it, great! They did what you wanted; however, if they don't, you can retarget them with ads bringing them straight back to your Core Offer sales page.

Obviously, as they progress through the funnel, you stop showing them the previous ads. For example, as soon as they've seen your "Super Awesome Blog Post", stop showing the ads that promote your blog post and instead show ads that promote your Lead Magnets. Once they grab one of your Lead Magnets, stop showing them those ads and only show ads that promote your Trip Wire. And so on.

As you can see, there's a lot you can do here and many things to try ... retargeting can make or break your campaigns!

What About Other Retargeting Platforms?

There are several 3rd party retargeting platforms out there like AdRoll, Perfect Audience, and Criteo ...

BUT! You're not going to pay them *any* attention!

You're going to stay focused on the 1 paid advertising source you selected way back during part 1!

There are so many features and options in both Facebook Ads Manager or Google Adwords that you have absolutely **ZERO reason** to dabble with a 3rd party tool.

Master your ***ONE*** platform first. Once you've really, *truly*, nailed it down ... ie. it's generating **profit** ... THEN, you can work on the other platform. Once you've mastered BOTH Facebook and Adwords *(will take you years)*, then ... sure, dabble with some 3rd party tools.

Ok?

Summary

Retargeting is a very powerful advertising method where you show ads to individuals that are on various audience lists ... lists that are created based on website activity, customer files, and engagement.

With these audience lists, you're able to create Lookalike or Similar Audiences to help expand your reach.

Combining retargeting with marketing automation (ie. emails) is a very powerful force.

There are a bunch of strategies you can employ with retargeting. Just use your head, look for "holes" in your marketing campaigns and "plug" them with retargeting ads.

Finally, don't mess with 3rd party retargeting tools until you've mastered BOTH Facebook and Google Adwords.

(part 5) How To Optimize Your Point Of Sale To Instantly Increase Revenue

You're at the grocery store, about to checkout, when a Snickers bar catches your eye ...

You throw it on the belt without giving it a second thought.

Then you think, "Hmm, I need something to wash it down!", so you place a Red Bull on the belt as well.

The grocery store just increased your Customer Lifetime Value (CLV).

Most physical stores are very, *very* good at positioning tantalizing products at the Point Of Sale (POS).

Products that get us to spend just a few more dollars with the business and increase our CLV.

So, physical stores are very good at this, but what happens when you're selling products and services online and you don't have your typical checkout with a register, clerk, and tantalizing products surrounding it?

You need to use some basic strategy and thoughtfulness + the right tools and you can increase CLV at the POS with ease!

This isn't just for Ecommerce!

Before moving on, I want to point out that this isn't just for Ecommerce!

All businesses, to include physical & digital products, services, coaches, consultants, and SaaS, should focus on optimizing their POS.

Consider things like warranties, additional support, bundling packages and offerings, or even partnering with other businesses for referrals and commissions.

There's no better time to increase CLV than when a customer already has his credit card out and is actively buying!

POS Optimization Strategies

Before getting into the strategies, I recommend reading ANNEX A on Value Ladders because it will help you structure your offerings in ways to make POS optimization a breeze!

1) Pricing Tiers, Packages, & Bundles

Pricing tiers, packages, and bundles are great ways to increase a customers' order size.

By using a bit of pricing psychology, you're able to present offers in a way that appear "too good to be true" while simultaneously increasing the amount of money a customer is about to hand you.

Take a look at this example from a2Hosting:

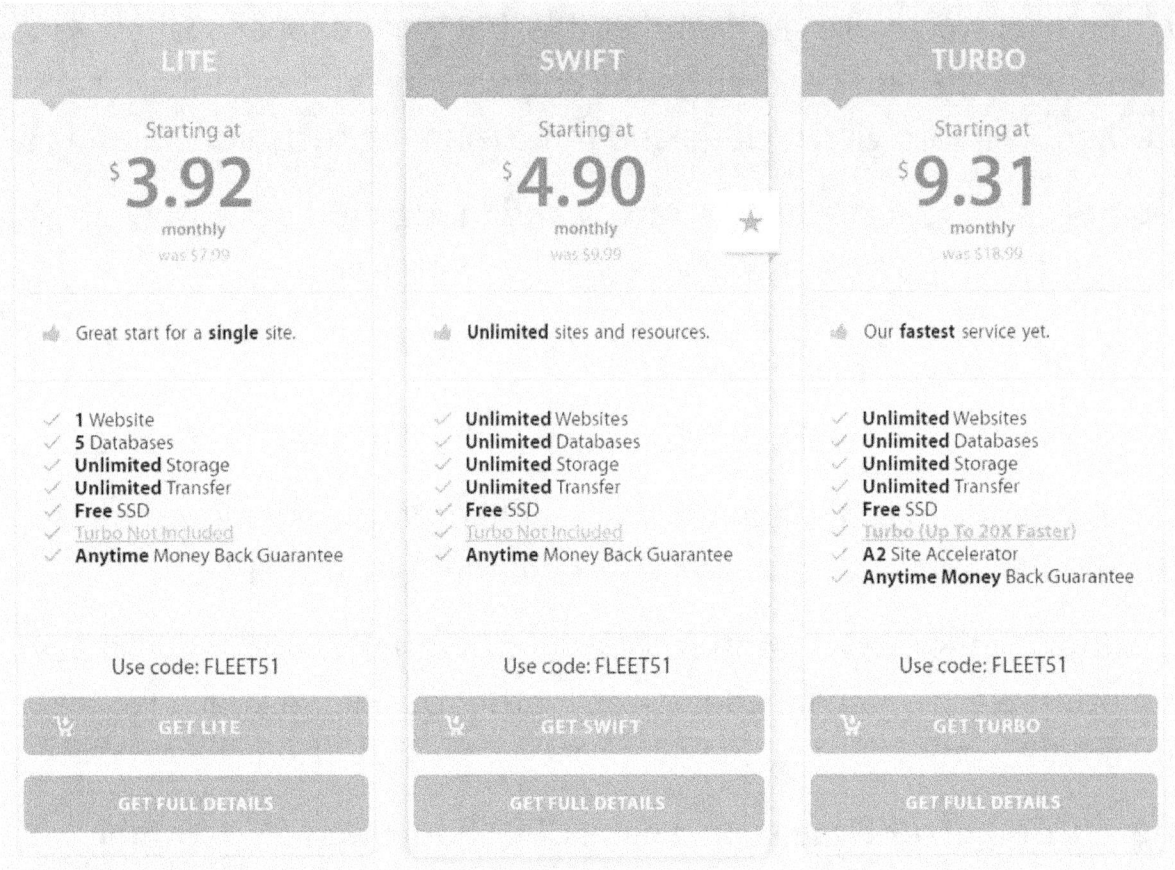

The "Swift" package is a no-brainer ... for less than a $1/mo more you get unlimited *everything*.

Why would anyone turn that down? No one would.

How about the "Turbo" package? It's nearly twice as much as the "Swift" package; however, it offers 20X faster speeds and the A2 Site Accelerator!

We all know speed is important and it's still less than $10/mo ... so, I might as well swing it, right?

Here's an example of a bundle of physical products:

Tide Amazing Laundry Bundle (68 Loads): Tide PODS,
Bounce Sheets and Downy Unstopables from Tide

⭐⭐⭐⭐½ ▾   286 customer reviews | 4 answered questions

If you're doing laundry, you typically need detergent, dryer sheets, and maybe a little fabric softener every now and then!

Plus, if you purchased these items individually, it would cost roughly 30% more which makes the bundle a no-brainer!

2) 1-Click Up-Sells

A 1-click up-sell is an offer presented immediately **AFTER** the customer has purchased something.

This makes the 1-click up-sell incredibly powerful because the individual has already inserted their payment information and all it takes is "1 click" to add another product/service to their order.

1-click up-sells are a key ingredient in the Classic Sales Funnel models discussed in part 6!

Here's an example:

Wait! Your order is not complete!

The Perfect Complement to Your Order
Add Survival Water Filter to your order now and receive 10% OFF!

Add To My Order

Order now and receive 10% off!

This Portable Water Filter Could Save Your Life

Could you survive without clean water?

- Have you wondered what would happen if you ran out of water?
- Do you ever go camping, hiking or backpacking?
- Are you looking for a backup plan if your water becomes contaminated?
- Want to upgrade your bug out bag for emergencies?

This Personal Water Filter is a Lightweight Water Filtration System (weighs less than 3 ounces)

This is the page and offer an individual is presented with *immediately after* purchasing a survival folding knife.

The individual is already in the mindset of "I need survival gear" and has already purchased one item, so when they're presented with another item that's discounted no-less, it's a no-brainer!

3) Order Bump

The infamous "order bump" has risen in popularity over the last year or so due to the fact it works!

It's so simple too, which makes it another no-brainer to implement.

Here's an example of an order bump:

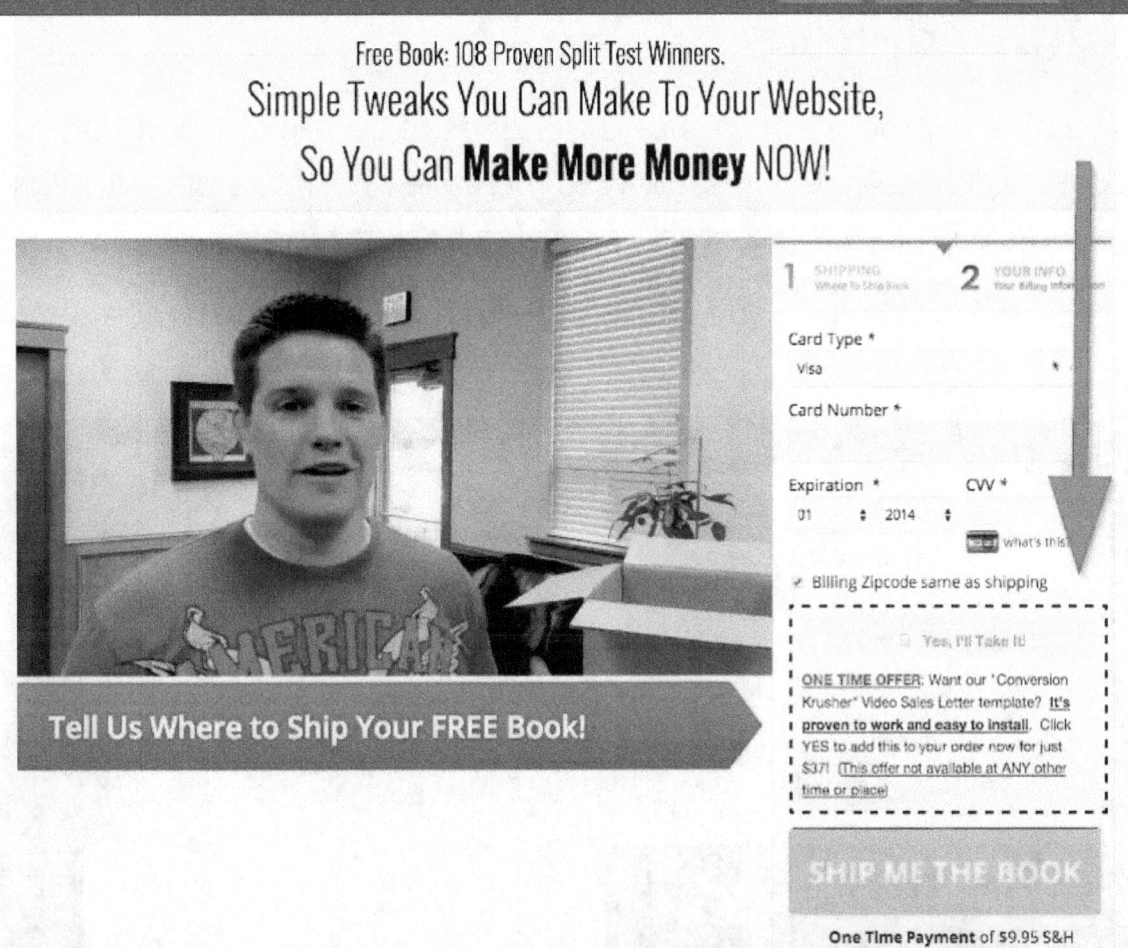

It's simply an additional, complementary offer made at checkout.

That's it!

The customer only has to tick a little box to add the product or service to their order.

It's actually quite similar to the 1-click up-sell; however, it's made right **before** the purchase as opposed to immediately **after** ... but, they're both 1-click!

The Order Bump is typically easier to implement than the 1-click up-sell. If you're having a hard time figuring out a way to do the 1-click up-sell, try searching for a way to add an order bump to your checkout process!

4) Subscriptions

If you offer a product or service that needs to be replenished - offering a subscription can be a great way to increase order size because it will automatically keep the customer coming back for more!

Here's an example of a subscription from the Youpreneur membership site:

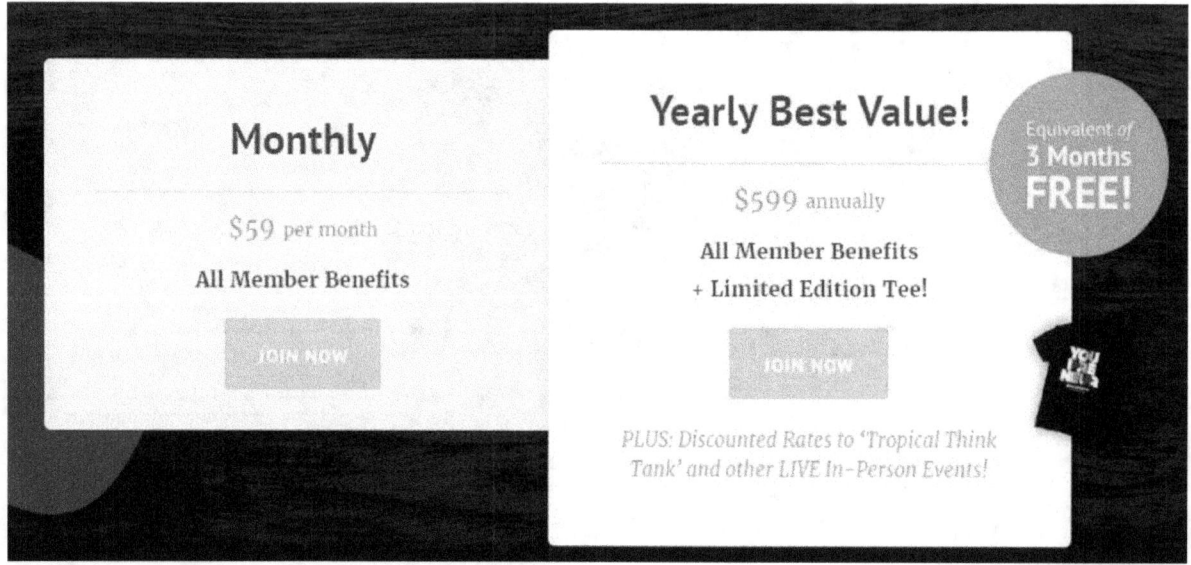

In order to stay a member of the community, you're charged $59/mo or $599/yr *(a bundle!)*.

Also note the yearly subscription is incentivized by offering the equivalent of 3 months free, a free t-shirt, and discounted rates to live events!

Here's another subscription example:

100% Fermented BCAAs Formula

Retail: $45.99

Online Store Price
$29.99

You Save $16.00 (34.79%)

BCAA Flavor:

Piña Colada ▼

HOW WOULD YOU LIKE TO ORDER?

⦿ One time Order

OR SAVE 5% WITH :

◯ Repeat Delivery every

30 days ▼

Why Choose Repeat Delivery?

IN STOCK

QTY 1 ▼

🛒 Add to Cart

🛒 INTERNATIONAL CUSTOMER CLICK HERE

Each container of the supplement contains 30 servings, which makes the "Repeat Delivery Every 30 Days" option incredibly tempting because I won't have to remember to go order more and by offering an extra 5% off, it becomes a no-brainer.

5) Order Bonuses & Rewards

Have you ever seen a message like this while shopping online:

"Spend just $5.91 more and get free shipping!"

Or ...

> Nice, you're only $72.01 away from getting FREE gift wrapping!

These are order bonuses/rewards used to entice customers to increase their order size in order to receive the incentive!

These are typically super simple to implement and freakin' work!

How To Implement

Implementing these various tweaks is not as hard as you might think.

For example, offering a package/bundle is as simple as bundling products/services you already offer.

Other options, like the 1-click up-sell, will depend on your platform. A quick Google search will likely yield some answers.

Conduct searches like ...

- [platform name] + 1-click up-sell *or* [platform name] + order bonuses. For example, shopify 1-click up-sell.

9 times out of 10, there is a plugin or add-on that will make whatever you're trying to accomplish possible.

Finally, there are various shopping carts like SamCart, ThriveCart, and ClickFunnels that integrate with many other platforms to make these tweaks possible.

Summary

Optimizing your Point Of Sale (POS) process is one of the most impactful areas to focus on because when a buyer is "in heat" they will keep buying until their needs are met or they run out of stuff to buy.

You never want the reason they stop buying to be that they've run out of stuff to buy. You need a plan and process in place to capitalize on the situation.

There are several strategies for optimizing your POS to include creating bundles, 1-click up-sells, order bumps, subscriptions, and bonuses/rewards.

Finding the right tool to make this happen can be as simple as installing a plugin or add-on or integrating with another shopping cart platform.

(part 6) How To Use Micro Sales Funnels To Convert More Leads Into Customers While Increasing CLV

In the beginning of this book, you started with understanding the fact **you're to act as a direct response marketer**.

Since you're a small business, you need to make sure every bit of marketing you do has a **specific & measurable goal.**

You have neither the time nor the money to waste on stuff that doesn't work.

Ya gotta make it count!

One of the best ways to make your marketing count is by having a strategy and *system* to sell your stuff.

We call these systems **Micro Sales Funnels.**

Use Micro Sales Funnels To Sell *EVERYTHING!*

Micro Sales Funnels are sometimes called Product/Service Sales Funnels because **they're strategically designed to help you sell specific product(s) and/or service(s).**

Micro Sales Funnels are used to sell both physical and digital products, services, coaching, consulting, SaaS, and even to drive foot traffic to brick & mortar businesses.

Micro Sales Funnels can, and should, be used to sell *everything*.

So, what do these magical, all powerful, systems look like?

It depends on what you're trying to sell, but here are a few different Micros Sales Funnel blueprints!

The Opt-in Funnel

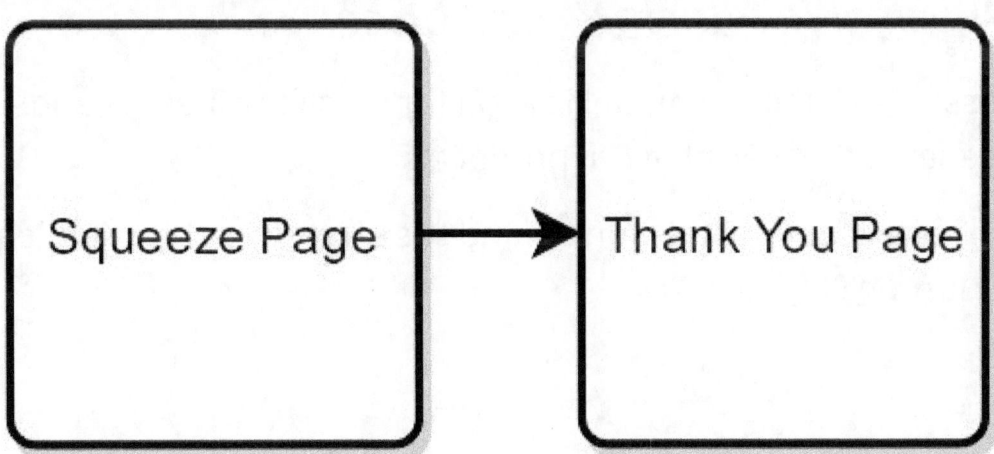

The Opt-in Funnel is the simplest Micro Sales Funnel; however, it's perfect for growing your email list and is typically the start of most other Micro Sales Funnel models.

You've seen a few examples of this funnel model in part 2 where we discussed using Squeeze Pages to convert paid traffic into email subscribers.

The Classic Sales Funnel (POS Funnel)

The Classic Sales Funnel is a Point Of Sale (POS) funnel because its purpose is to increase Customer Lifetime Value (CLV) at the POS by offering additional products/services as the customer goes through the checkout process.

This is accomplished through the implementation of various tactics like Order Bumps and 1-Click Up-sells or One-Time-Offers (OTO) & Down-sells. *(yup, we talked about these in* <u>part 5</u>*)*

The structure of the Classic Sales Funnel can vary based upon what you're offering via up-sells (OTOs) and down-sells ... there's no "defined" structure; however, below are a few common Classic Sales Funnels.

The Physical Products Sales Funnel

This Classic Sales Funnel model is ideal for small businesses and entrepreneurs that sell physical products.

For a full breakdown of this funnel and the strategy behind it, please check out <u>ANNEX E</u>.

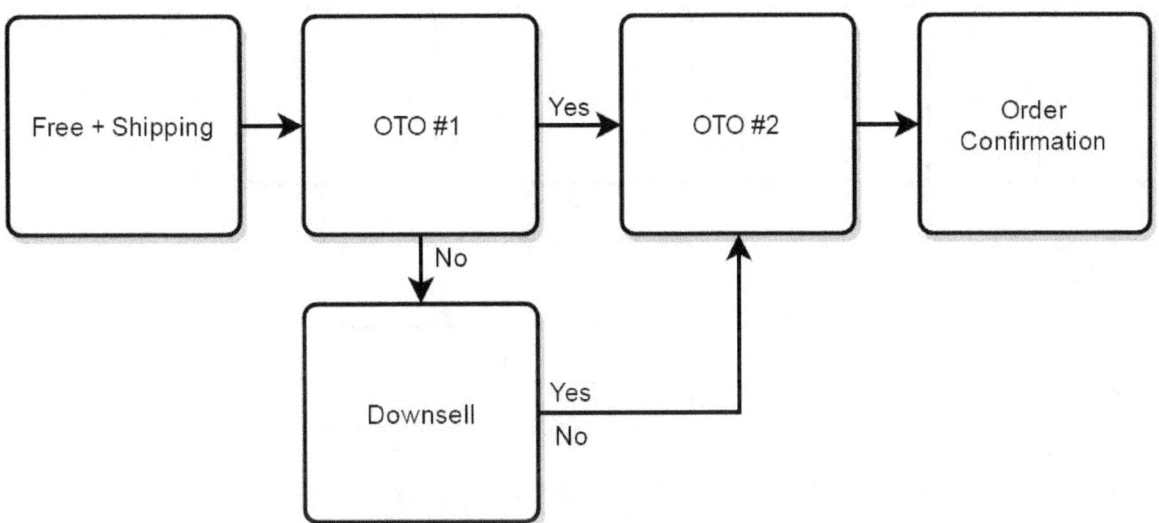

The Digital Products Sales Funnel

This Classic Sales Funnel model is ideal for small businesses and entrepreneurs that sell offer digital/info products.

For a full breakdown of this funnel and the strategy behind it, please check out ANNEX F.

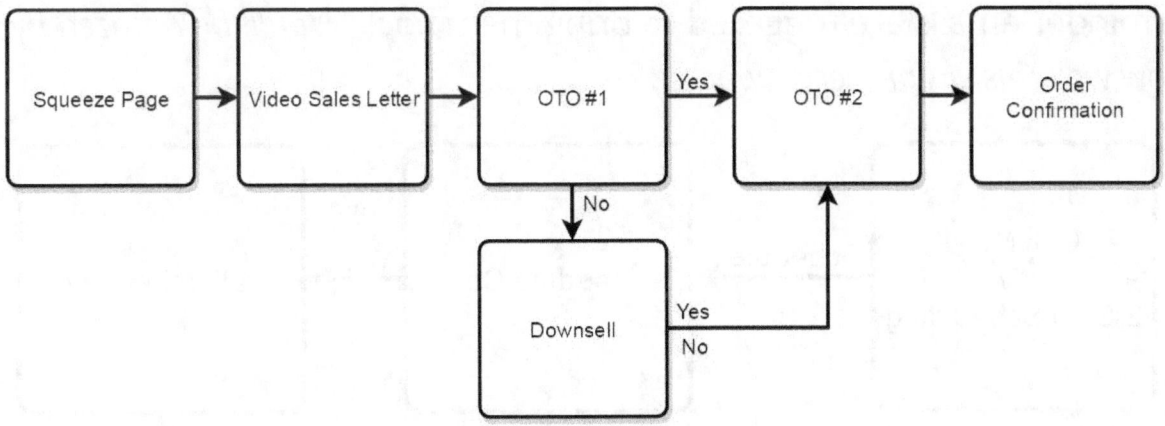

The "Book" Sales Funnel

This Classic Sales Funnel model is ideal for service based businesses, coaches, and consultants that have a book to offer as their front-end and services, coaching, and/or consulting to offer on the back-end.

For a full breakdown of this funnel and the strategy behind it, please check out ANNEX G.

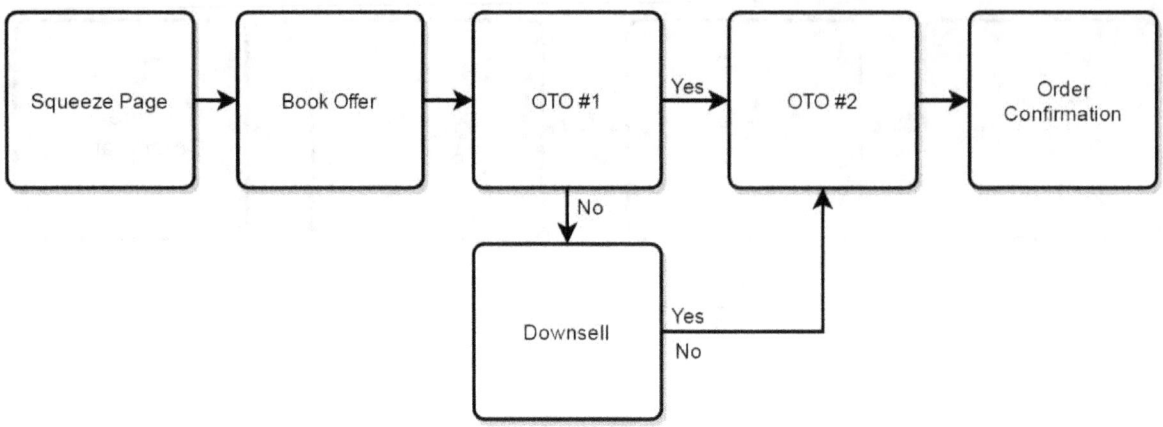

The High-End "Call/Application" Sales Funnel

This simple, yet effective sales funnel is ideal for getting people on the phone and/or to fill out an application for high-end services, coaching, consulting, and mastermind groups.

The power of this funnel comes from offering visitors two ways to get in touch with you - they can call now or schedule a call for later.

If they choose to schedule a call for later, but don't go through with it, reminder emails are triggered to bring them back. *(You'll be amazed by how well this simple series works!)*

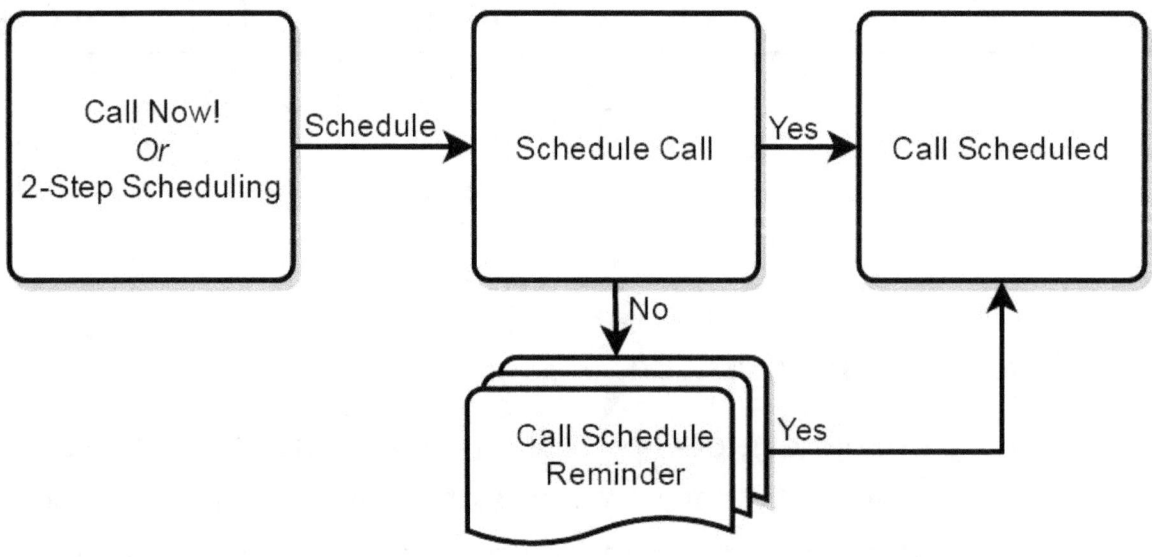

The Product Launch Sales Funnel

The Product Launch Sales Funnel is designed to sell high value courses and training packages.

It combines emails with video content "dripped" out over a few days that pre-sell the course you're going to offer and culminates with the "launching" of your product.

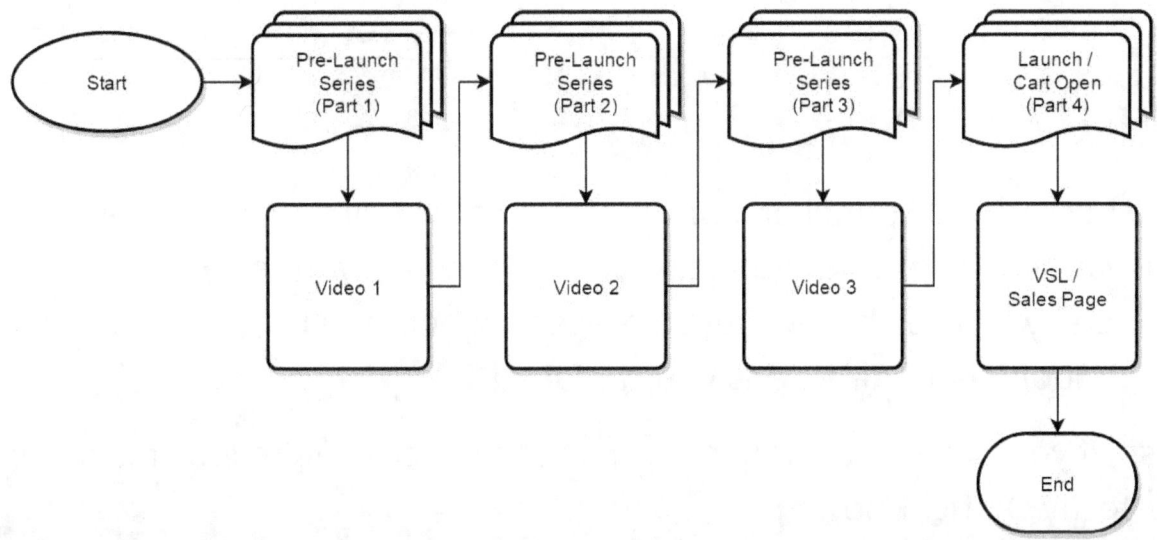

The Autowebinar Sales Funnel

Webinars are virtual seminars where you're able to sell high priced products and services.

They're great because you're able to have people's attention for about 90 minutes which gives you ample time to gain their trust and present your offer.

An autowebinar, frequently called an "evergreen webinar", is a webinar that runs automatically 24 hours a day, constantly selling for you.

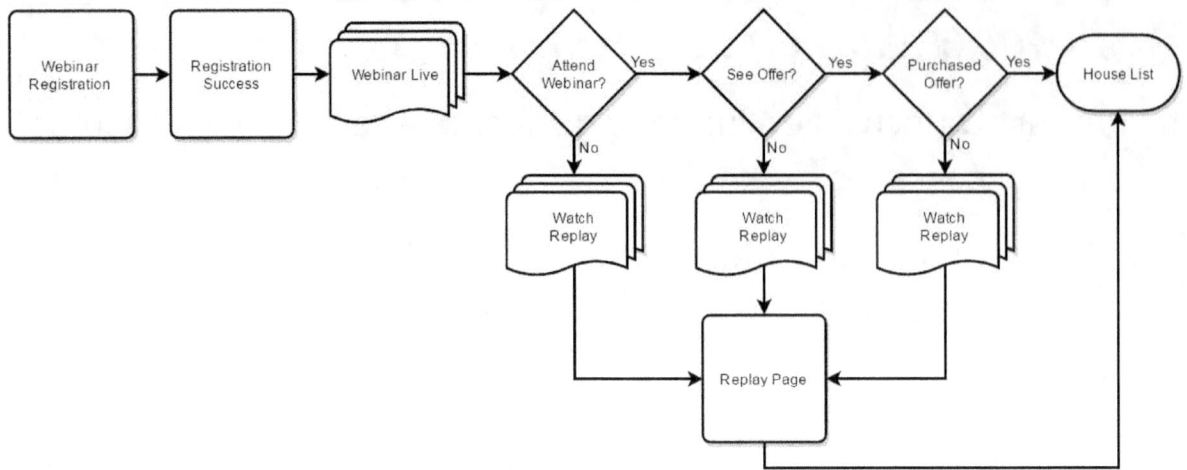

Other Micro Sales Funnels

The Micro Sales Funnel blueprints shared above are a small sample of the various Micro Sales Funnels you can create ... you're by no means limited by what's above. They're presented here to give you ideas and inspiration about directions you can head.

Also, if you don't quite understand what the heck you're looking at, it's perfectly OK right now.

The key thing I want you to remember is that **the sole purpose of a Micro Sales Funnel is to** _**help you sell specific product(s) and/or service(s).**_

Ways To Enter A Micro Sales Funnel

Hopefully you've read the previous sections of this book and you already know how to get people into your Micro Sales Funnels; however, if not - here's a recap!

Organic Traffic

Individuals can enter your Micro Sales Funnels by opt-ing in through an opt-in form on your site. (part 2)

This is accomplished by offering a Lead Magnet on topic X, which leads them into a Micro Sales Funnel that tries to sell a product/service people interested in topic X would want to buy.

Paid Traffic

If you're paying for traffic, you **better** have a Micro Sales Funnel in place! (part 2)

If you don't have a way to quickly recoup your ad spend, you're going to hurt your business.

After all, **you're a direct response marketer** ... *right?*

Everything you do needs to have specific and measurable purpose.

The point of your marketing is to make you more money.

Marketing Automation

In part 3 we discussed using marketing automation to gauge our subscribers' interests.

I showed you this diagram:

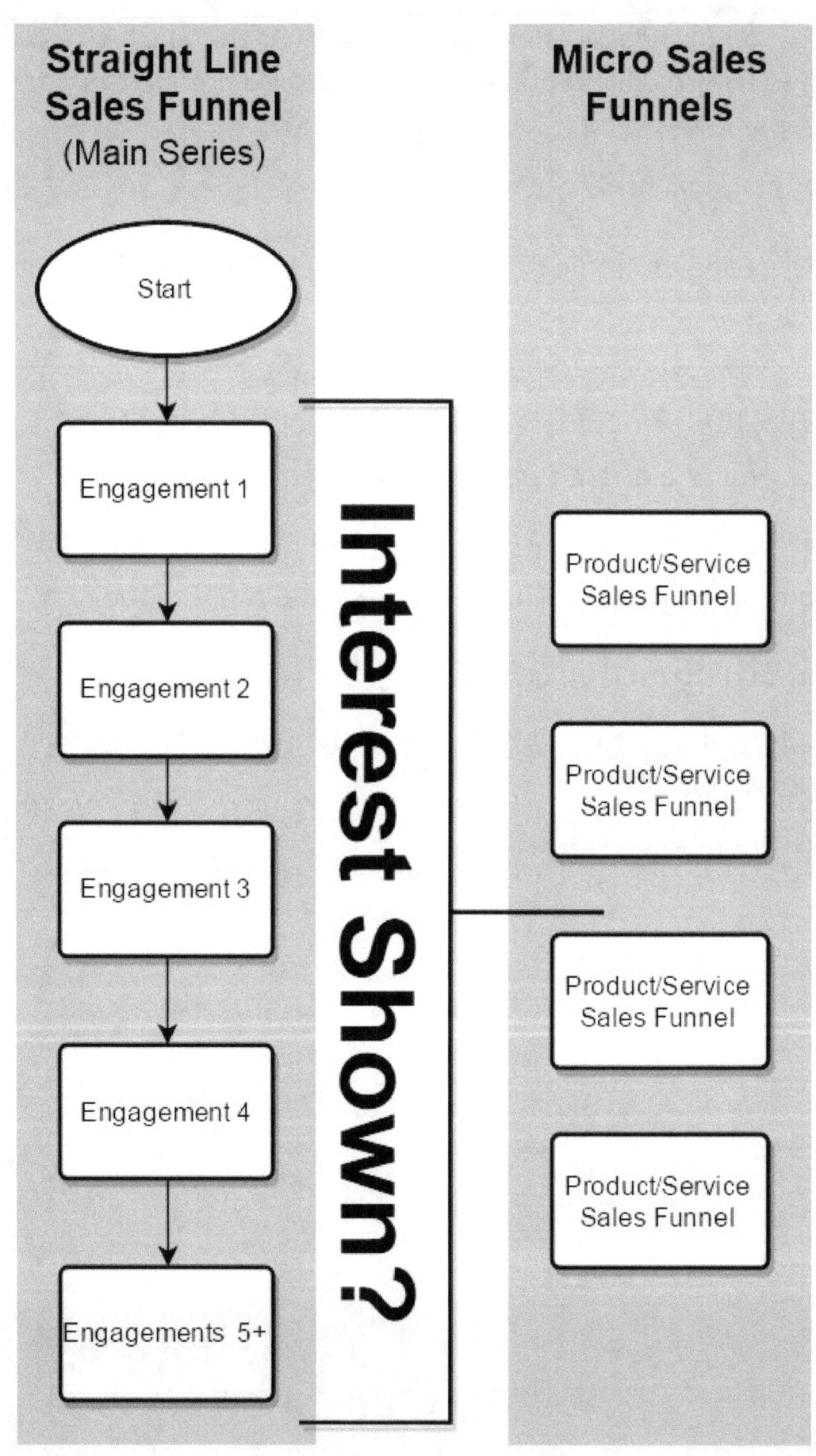

To recap, the left-hand side is a Straight Line Sales Funnel or "Main Series".

Its purpose is to build and maintain a relationship with your subscribers by sending great content while **simultaneously segmenting them based on their interests.**

When a subscriber shows interest in a particular topic (ie. they click a link), they're automatically entered into a Micro Sales Funnel that attempts to sell a product or service they will likely buy.

Retargeting

Retargeting is another great way to get individuals into your Micro Sales Funnels. (part 4)

You can also use retargeting to "guide" individuals through your Micro Sales Funnels because not everyone is going to read every email you send them. However, if you send an email AND retarget them with relevant ads ... they won't be able to avoid your message!

Summary

You NEED to use Micro Sales Funnels.

There is no better way to convert leads into paying customers while simultaneously increasing their Customer Lifetime Value.

There are many Micro Sales Funnel blueprints to choose from; however, the design you choose will depend on what you're trying to sell ... not all Micro Sales Funnels are designed to sell the same stuff.

Some are better at selling more expensive training, courses, and services while others are excellent at selling low priced (<$100) products.

Finally, getting people to enter your Micro Sales Funnels is as simple as sending traffic to it!

Take Action!

Now What?

Books are great.

They teach you so much nifty stuff and usually leave you feeling like you've accomplished a great task...

Then reality sets in and you realize you've produced nothing.

Would you trust a brain surgeon who has only read a book on brain surgery? Someone who hasn't at least practiced on cow brains ... *or something?*

I know I wouldn't.

Not that digital marketing for small businesses and entrepreneurs is as complex as brain surgery, but it still requires practice.

It still requires work.

You're not going to multiply your business by simply consuming.

You have to take action.

If the digital marketing strategy covered in this book sounds interesting and logical to you ...

It's the same exact strategy taught in **The Sales Funnel Training Vault** ... it's just, in there, we go into a lot more detail and cover all the technical steps as well.

Learn More: **https://crazyeyemarketing.com/join/**

If you have any questions, never hesitate to send me an email at nathan@crazyeyemarketing.com.

All the best to you and your business!

Annexes

ANNEX A: The Value Ladder Concept

This is a blog post from https://crazyeyemarketing.com/blog/how-to-create-a-value-ladder-for-your-sales-funnel/. I think it will be incredibly helpful for those that are struggling to figure out what to try and sell with regard to up-sells, down-sells, and cross-sells.

How To Create A Value Ladder For Your Sales Funnel

This Is Important!

Before charging head first into sales funnel creation, you **_need_** to take the time to map out your value ladder – your products and services mapped In ascending order of value and price.

The Value Ladder

General Concept

As people "ascend" your value ladder, they're offered more value; however, this value comes at a price ($).

Note: Value doesn't necessarily mean "more". You can also provide greater value by saving people time.

Tiers

Your value ladder doesn't necessarily need 5 tiers as the diagram above shows. Offering multiple value tiers at various price points gives you more opportunity to give your customers exactly what they need.

Lead Magnet

The freebies you give away to grow your list and get people in the door.

- **Price:** Free
- **Goals:** Qualify & Capture Leads
- **Examples:** Checklist, Guide, Video, Free Sample, Trial, Coupon

Initial Offer

The low-end products you offer that ideally cover the cost of advertising and "prove" the lead has enough "pain" that they're willing to spend money to resolve it. Many times you'll see "Free plus Shipping" offers.

- **Price:** < $10
- **Goals:** Re-Capture Ad Spend & Qualify Customers
- **Examples:** Book, Course, Product

1st Tier

The low-mid range products and services you offer generate profit while simultaneously building trust with the customer as they receive more value from you and your business.

- **Price:** < $100
- **Goals:** Increase Profits & Build Trust
- **Examples:** Course, Productized Service, Product

2nd Tier

The high-mid range products and services you offer generate profit, ideally recurring revenue, from membership and continuity programs.

- **Price:** < $1,000
- **Goals:** Increase Profits & Recurring
- **Examples:** Course, Membership, Custom Service, Product

Top Tier

The biggest and best product/service you have!

- **Price:** > $1,000
- **Goals:** Increase Profits & Recurring
- **Examples:** Done For You Service, Masterminds

Product Based Businesses

I know what you're thinking, "A value ladder sounds nice, especially for digital and service based businesses, but I sell physical products and things just aren't "fitting"."

Don't worry, I've got you covered!

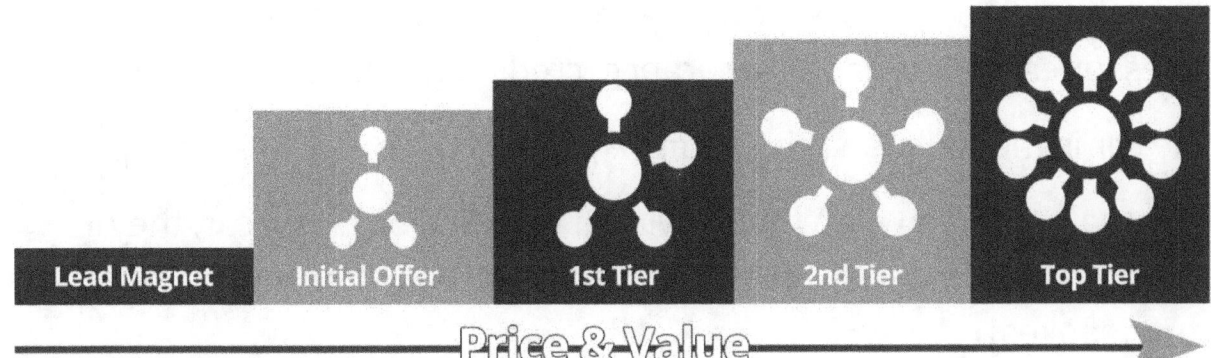

Incorporate The Hub And Spoke Model

The "hub" is the core product and the "spokes" are all the accessories and peripherals that "enhance" the core product.

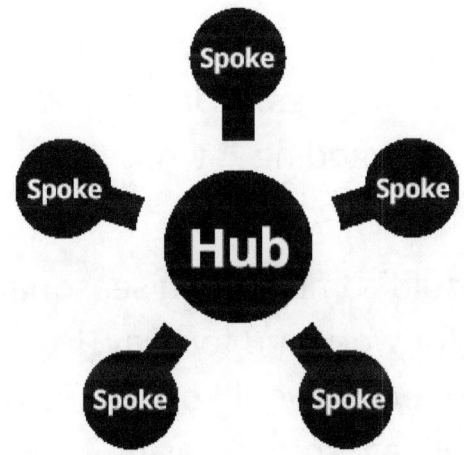

Many times, businesses that sell physical products can't "ascend" customers the same way digital and service-based businesses can.

For example, if you sell cars, you can develop and give away a lead magnet and you can likely come up with an initial offer for under $10 (ie. a car buying guide). However, after those first two steps ... there's not much ... you gotta sell a car!

You're not going to try and sell a motorized bicycle, then a scooter, then a motorcycle, then a car, then a nicer car, then an even nicer car *(at least not in one sitting)*. It simply doesn't work that way; however, after the individual purchases a car, they're going to need a lot more stuff – accessories, maintenance, insurance, credit, etc. for years to come.

The car is the "hub" and the additive products/services are the "spokes".

Eventually, *ideally*, when the individual is ready for a new car, they'll ascend to the next level, get a new car (hub), and start buying more stuff (spokes).

Another Example (Retail)

A few years ago, when I first came across the value ladder concept, I tried to apply it to an ecommerce business that also had a brick & mortar location. This particular retailer sold women's clothing – dresses, to be exact.

They offered many different types of dresses from seasonal, to professional, to formal, to wedding ... what "appeared" to be a natural ladder ... and it was, somewhat.

Many times, women would come in for a seasonal dress and leave with two or more dresses – for work and for play. However, there were many occasions where women would only need one type of dress for one specific occasion – ie. a formal occasion.

This was where the hub and spoke model came into play as there are a TON of accessories with formal wear – shoes, bags, jewelry, makeup, etc.

Let's stick with the woman that came in and purchased a formal dress. In this case, a wedding dress, even though it's "technically" the next step in the value ladder, doesn't have to be the next step ... *especially* if she's not engaged and/or doesn't have a boyfriend *(or girlfriend, whatever floats your boat – not the point)*.

The point is, there are likely many seasons and occasions for more dresses (hubs) and accessories (spokes) between now and then that can be capitalized upon, if done correctly.

If it makes sense to ascend people up your ladder, ascend them. If not, be sure to incorporate enough spokes!

Offer Continuity

Often, customers will not ascend your entire value ladder *ever*, much less in one sitting. For those that do ascend, it can take weeks, months, or even years to ascend to the next level.

This is where offering a continuity program or recurring offer comes into play because it helps **accelerate ascension** while increasing **capitalization**.

For example:

- A car dealership can offer oil changes. Cars need oil changes, making this is a natural offer.

- A dress shop can offer a subscription service where every month or season they send out the appropriate style of sunglasses for maybe $10/mo. Not only will this sell more sunglasses, but it serves as a reminder to the customer that they need a new dress for the new season!

- Digital products businesses can offer a community and/or premium support as a recurring offer.

- Dentists offer 6 month check-ups.

Bundles & Down-sells

Bundles and down-sells come in handy, especially if you're stuck or are truly limited in what you have to offer.

Let's say you sell 10 different products, that all cost $30, and don't have any additional accessories, even ones you could offer as an affiliate. *(unlikely, but this is a hypothetical!)*

Could you create bundles of these products? Maybe a 3 pack, 5 pack, and 10 pack? There's your ladder!

For example:

- This concept can be applied to businesses that only offer one thing, for example, a soft serve ice cream shop. Beyond up-selling more ice cream, they can offer a punch card for $X that grants the holder 5 cups, 10 cups, 20 cups, etc. at various price breaks.

- Barber shops can also take advantage of the bundling concept. While many offer other services like shaves, dyeing, massages, etc., that can be bundled into packages, they can also bundle visits onto punch cards in a similar fashion to the ice cream shops.

- Here at Crazy Eye Marketing, we offer courses and resources individually and as a bundle we call The Vault. (https://crazyeyemarketing.com/join/)

Down-Sell Mega Tip!

One of the best ways to help people ascend your value ladder quickly is to reduce the entry price to the next tier.

How?

Payment plans!

Let's say your 1st Tier product costs $97 and your 2nd Tier product costs $247, you can split your 2nd Tier product into 3 easy payments of $93.67!

Doing this makes the 2nd Tier product a no-brainer as it costs less than the 1st Tier product (at least for *today* – which is what the mind tends to focus on [instant gratification]).

Reverse The Entire Ladder!

This entire time I've been talking about having customers *ascend* your value ladder, but what if you reversed it and had them *descend?!*

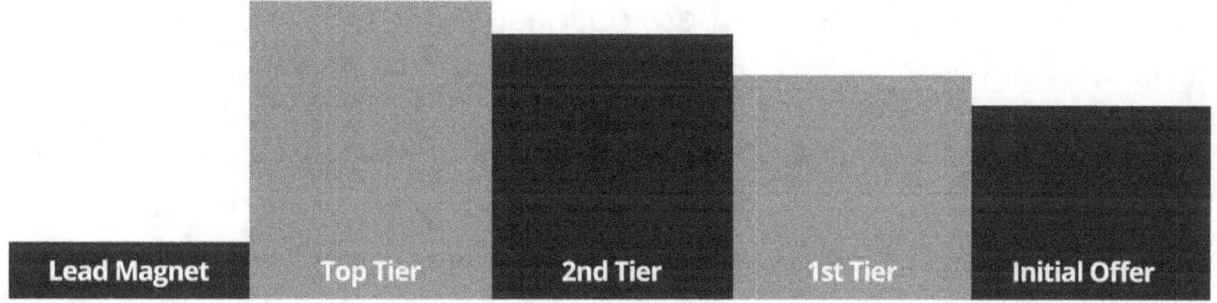

You still start with a lead magnet in order to attract and qualify leads, but then you'll go straight into presenting your top tier offer!

If they're not interested, try a "down-sell mega tip" (payment plan). If that doesn't work, move to the 2nd Tier offer. If that doesn't work, try a payment plan. If that doesn't work, move to the 1st Tier offer, and so on.

Who knows, maybe implementing a reversed value ladder will yield greater results ... it's certainly worth trying!

ANNEX B: What Is A Lead Magnet? & 10 Examples

A lead magnet is an incentive, or "bribe", to convince an individual to give you their contact information.

You see lead magnets everywhere online in the form of discounts, contests, eBooks, checklists, video courses, etc.

But, lead magnets don't exist solely online. Think about all of those "member" cards you have on your keyring for grocery stores, gas stations, and department stores. They offer you "points" in exchange for your contact information.

Think about store specific credit cards. Every time I walk into a Target, I'm offered one of their credit cards in exchange for 5% off all of my purchases.

Obviously, as a business owner / marketer - having either a points card or credit card that tracks your customers' purchasing behavior would be phenomenal. You could tailor your marketing efforts incredibly effectively.

Some kind of card that tracks purchases would be an ideal lead magnet; however, those options might not be practical for your business. In this annex, I'll address several lead magnet ideas you can use in your business.

A Lead Magnet Has Three Parts

I'm not going to go into too much detail in this section, I just want to point out the fact that a lead magnet is more than having a simple little giveaway.

You will also need a page, or a section on your page that does a great job promoting your lead magnet and collecting the contact information. This type of page is often referred to as a landing page or squeeze page.

You will also need traffic to your landing page and lead magnet. Traffic can be generated any number of ways and without it, your lead magnet will not be successful.

To summarize, a lead magnet is made up of:

- The giveaway (coupon, eBook, checklist, course, trial, etc)

- The landing page (to promote the giveaway and collect the contact info)

- The traffic (from advertising)

These Days...

Back in the good 'ol days (like 2 years ago), the bigger your lead magnet - the better. It used to be that a 200 page eBook was better than a 100 page eBook, which was obviously better than a measly 50 page eBook.

However, over time, people came to realize that they weren't even reading a 10 page eBook, much less a 200 page one. So, they stopped giving up their contact information in exchange for such massive eBooks.

These days, "quick answers" work best.

A single coupon, a 1 page checklist, and a 5 minute video tend to outperform a 200 page eBook.

This is great news for you, the lead magnet creator! Now, you don't have to worry about compiling a massive lead magnet!

10 Lead Magnet Examples

Below are 10 lead magnet examples. Of course, this list is not all inclusive, but it should help you get started.

1. Coupon / Discount

A coupon can drive people to your store, and/or to make a purchase. A coupon can be the deciding factor between someone going to your store or one of your competitors.

For example, if someone searches "ecig coupon chester va" - and you have a coupon readily available - you'll get that customer AND their contact info.

I recommend every physical store, that sells a commodity, to have a coupon available and don't hesitate to pay to advertise that lead magnet in order to get ahead of your competitors.

2. Checklist / Step-list

A checklist can be a great lead magnet, if there is some sort of process that can by systematized and helpful to your audience.

For example, if listing a product on Amazon, there are certain steps one has to go through every time to list their product. There's the title, description, pictures, etc.

Offering people a checklist or step-by-step instructions can help them accomplish the task they set out to perform.

3. eBook

Even though I "bashed" eBooks a few paragraphs ago - they can still work as lead magnets. It simply depends on what your audience wants.

One tip, if you decide to go the eBook route - break it into small sections, and make each section independent of the others.

For example, if you have an eBook about fly fishing - one section could be about flies, one about equipment, and one about locations. This way, a reader can quickly find the answer they're looking for without having to read a massive eBook.

4. Contest / Raffle Entry

You see these all the time and they're self-explanatory, so I won't go into much detail here.

The good part about these; however, is they can go viral. For example, in order to enter the contest, you must give up your contact information AND share the contest!

5. Free Trial

Free trials can work wonderfully.

For example, many SaaS companies give free month long trials to their software.

Also, gyms are another prime example of a business giving a free month long membership - heck, I just had one!

6. Video Course

Video courses and the online learning market are booming right now. If you're able to offer a video course that teaches someone, something to make their job easier - it can be a successful lead magnet.

7. Notification of Future Products

Some people enjoy being on the cutting edge and having the latest and greatest. They're more than willing to give up their contact information in exchange for being notified when a product is launched.

For example, my wife wants a FitBit. However, the color she wants has not been released - guess what - we're on their email list waiting to be notified when the color is launched.

8. Webinars

Webinars are essentially online seminars that both teach and sell to its attendants. This make them a great choice - the attendants learn something and you make money!

You can also automate webinars which enables you to record them once to be used again and again.

While there are many webinar strategies out there, one of the best ones is the Perfect Webinar by Russell Brunson. You can learn more about it at https://perfectwebinarsecrets.com/get-it-free.

9. Flowcharts / Frameworks

I hate to say this, but people are lazy and if something's hard - they won't do it.

If you're able to give an individual step-by-step directions in a logical flow, they'll eat it up!

My favorite flowchart software is draw.io. It's free, web based, and syncs nicely with Google Drive.

10. Mind Maps

Similar to flowcharts, mind maps are a simple way to visually organize information.

They tend to be 1-page and loaded with great information that can be quickly and easily consumed.

Below is a link to a video on how to make one from scratch in about 20 minutes!

How To Create A Great Lead Magnet FAST (from scratch!)

Here's the video: https://www.youtube.com/watch?v=fLqjs6MLrzU

Tools Used:

- Pinterest
- Coggle

Closing Tips:

Developing a lead magnet doesn't have to be too time consuming or difficult. It's not a "the bigger the better" type of thing. For example, a 100 page eBook - might not do as well as a one page checklist.

So, here are a few tips to set you up for success:

- **Be specific.** This is referring to both the lead magnet and the results.

   - Bad Example: 50 page eBook called, "Learn To Be A Champion Cyclist"

- o Good Example: 1 page checklist called, "8 Steps To Breaking 60 Minutes In The 40k"

- **Delivers immediate gratification.** People want answers to their problems <u>now</u>. They don't want to have to wait for the answer. Think of a way to keep it short and sweet, so they're immediately fulfilled and have a direction to go in.

  - o Obviously, breaking 60 minutes in a 40k bike race will require months of hard training; however, the 1 page checklist will immediately provide the direction for someone to go in.

- **One Promise.** Keep it simple. This follows with the previous bullets - you don't have to create the bible on bike racing. You don't have to address nutrition, clothing, training plans, bike setups, etc.

  - o The lead magnet should provide <u>one answer</u> to <u>one problem</u>.

ANNEX C: 8 Opt-In Form Examples You Can Implement With Ease

Most people have a love/hate relationship with opt-in forms.

As a visitor to a website, they can be incredibly annoying ... especially when they keep popping over what you're trying to read.

But, as the site owner, we know those pop-up opt-in forms tend to work. So, we keep showing them.

This creates an interesting dichotomy, but that's beyond the scope of this particular annex.

In this annex we'll talk about opt-in form tools, triggers, and types.

Opt-in Form Tools

You really only need one opt-in form tool and the one you use is determined by your platform.

WordPress | Thrive Leads

If your website is powered by WordPress, the best opt-in form plugin you can grab is Thrive Leads.

Why? It's incredibly powerful.

It allows you to build any type of opt-in form you can imagine, conduct split tests, page targeting, and beyond.

Any Other Platform | OptinMonster

If your website is powered by anything other than WordPress (ie. Shopify, Big Commerce, custom coded, etc.), the best opt-in form tool you can grab is OptinMonster.

It's essentially just like ThriveLeads; however, it can work *anywhere* ... which is great for sites that aren't powered by WordPress!

Note: Since OptinMonster works *anywhere*, it will work on WordPress too. If you run sites on multiple platforms, it would be best to just get OptinMonster.

Display Triggers

Both, Thrive Leads and OptinMonster have very similar triggers. While the particular name of the trigger may change - SmartExit+ vs. Exit Intent Technology - the general function of the trigger remains the same (ie. display upon exit).

Below are the four triggers functions both opt-in tools offer.

Timed Triggers

From immediately to 30 seconds or more, you can choose when your opt-in form shows itself.

If you don't have a reason to have your opt-in form display immediately, a good rule of thumb is to give the visitor about 10 seconds to get into your material before greeting them with the opt-in form.

Exit Triggers

An exit trigger can only occur on desktop and it's when a visitor's cursor leaves the browser window.

Typically, the only reason the cursor would leave the browser window is because they're about to hit the "back" button or navigate off your site.

As a last-ditch effort, you can display an opt-in form to try and collect the visitor's contact information.

Click Triggers

Click triggers are really popular because they show intent, which typically leads to much higher conversion rates.

Instead of blindly displaying an opt-in form after 10 seconds, a click triggered opt-in form is displayed after an individual clicks a link, button, or image.

Scroll Triggers

Scroll triggers are used to display opt-in forms after an individual has scrolled down a percentage of a page or past a certain point.

For example, you could have an opt-in form display after the visitor has scrolled down 75% of the page. Ideally, this means they've read 75% of the page, are therefore highly interested in what you're talking about, and more apt to opt-in.

Types Of Opt-In Forms

Pop-up LightBox

The "classic" opt-in form.

Although they're kind of annoying, you see this type of opt-in form everywhere ... because they work!

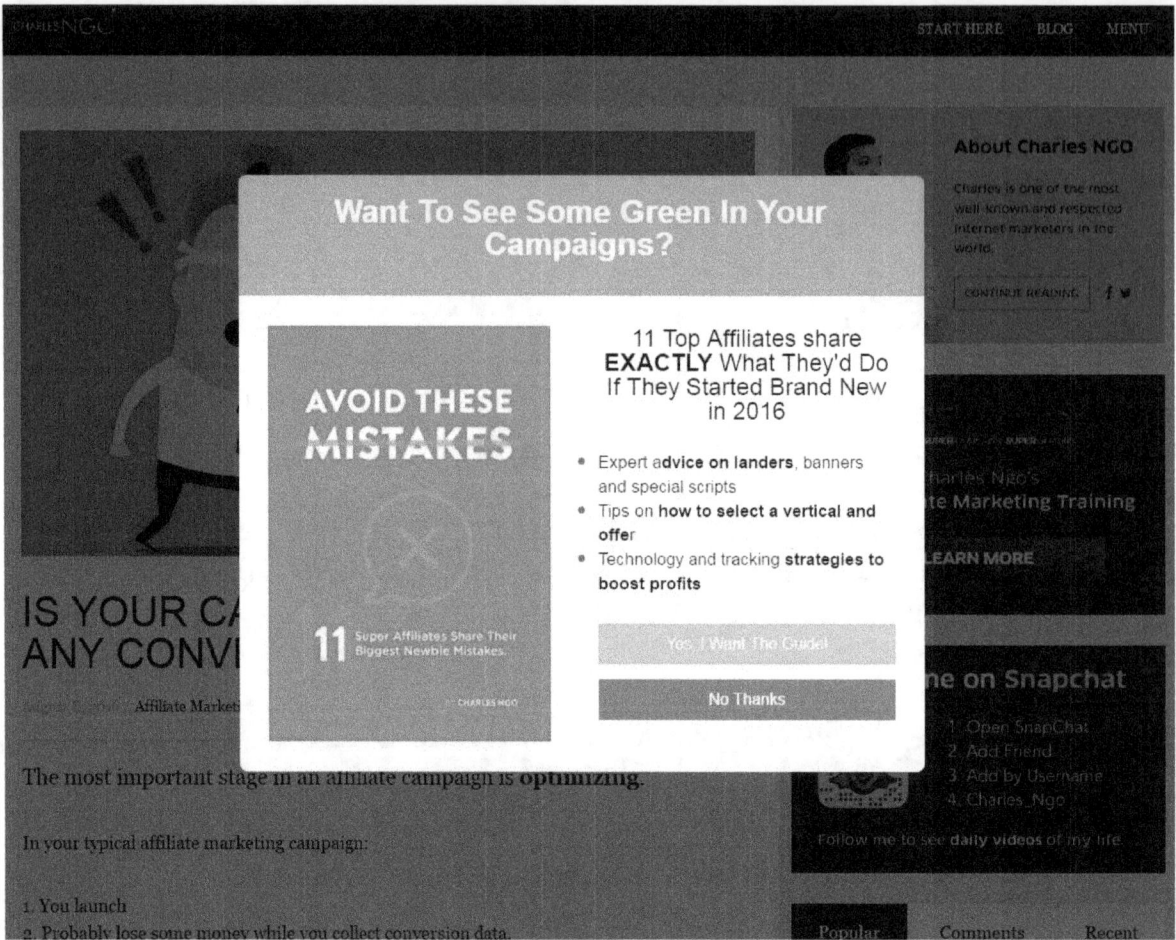

Example From <u>Charles NGO</u>

In-Line / After Post

These opt-in forms "blend" in with the content.

They're nice because they don't hinder the visitor's experience, yet they still provide an easy way to opt-in for your lead magnet.

- 292 new email subscribers

Worth it? I think so. Plus those numbers will continue to climb as this pillar piece of content matures and collects more traffic.

But more importantly, the article was actually a ton of fun to work on. Each day Bryn would come home and I'd be like, "Guess what new platform I discovered today! Did you know there's an Airbnb for boats??"

And the next exciting piece is the post has inspired a new book project. Stay tuned for more info on that in the coming weeks and months!

Your Turn

What happens when you create "epic" content? I think the more pressing question is what happens when you don't.

In-Line / After Post

Join the Nation!

Free Report: The 5 Fastest Ways to Make More Money

Join today and download the free report *The 5 Fastest Ways to Make More Money*, plus get actionable tips and insight to advance your side hustle each week.

Name:

Email:

JOIN NOW - IT'S FREE!

Related Posts:

MY FACEBOOK ADS

Example From [Side Hustle Nation](#)

Widgets / Side Bar

Very similar to in-line opt-in forms because they're "just there." They don't pop-in or slide, but are "just there" in the sidebar or widget area of a site.

Example From <u>My Wife Quit Her Job</u>

Ribbons/Bar

These opt-in bars or ribbons go across the top or bottom of the page and are typically "locked in place" (they scroll with the page).

These are great because they allow you to share your Lead Magnet without being obnoxious by popping up a lightbox or a screen overlay.

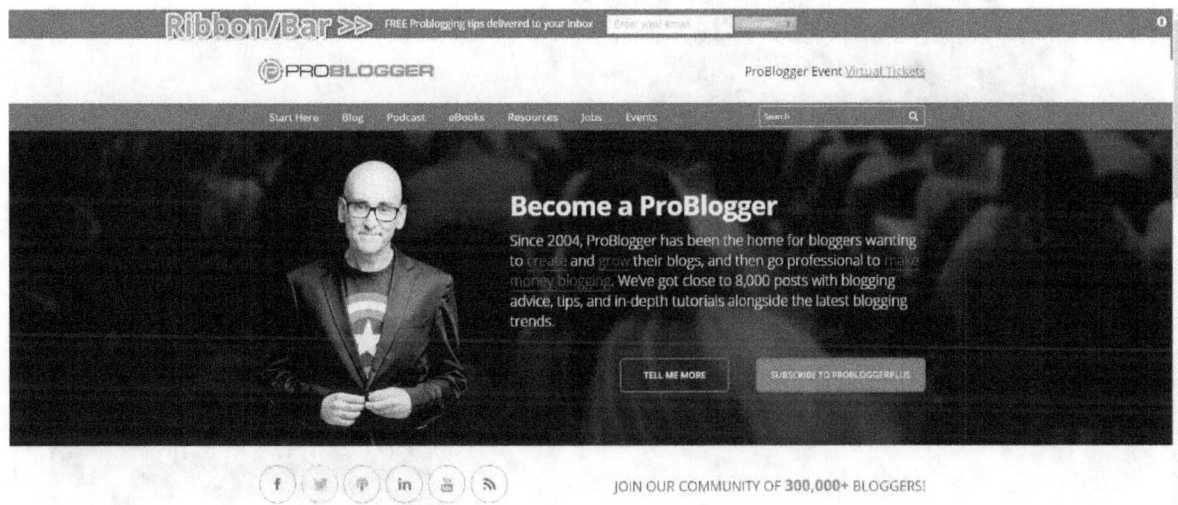

Example From <u>ProBlogger</u>

Slide-In

This type of opt-in form "slides" into view. They're typically in the corners of pages; however, they can take over an entire side too!

These are great because they can be fairly unobtrusive while still catching people's attention.

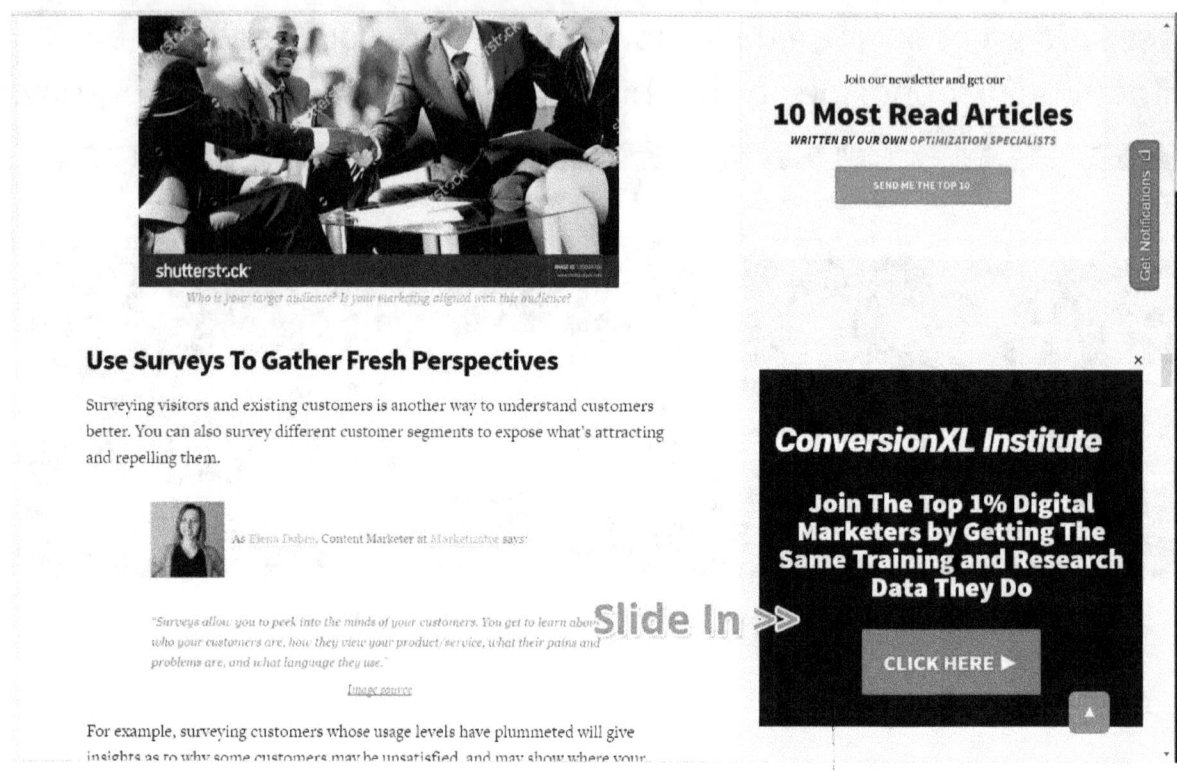

Example From <u>ConversionXL</u>

Screen Overlays/Takeovers

This type of opt-in form takes over the entire page, leaving the individual two options - to opt-in or to **close it**.

These tend to work very well because you can't miss 'em.

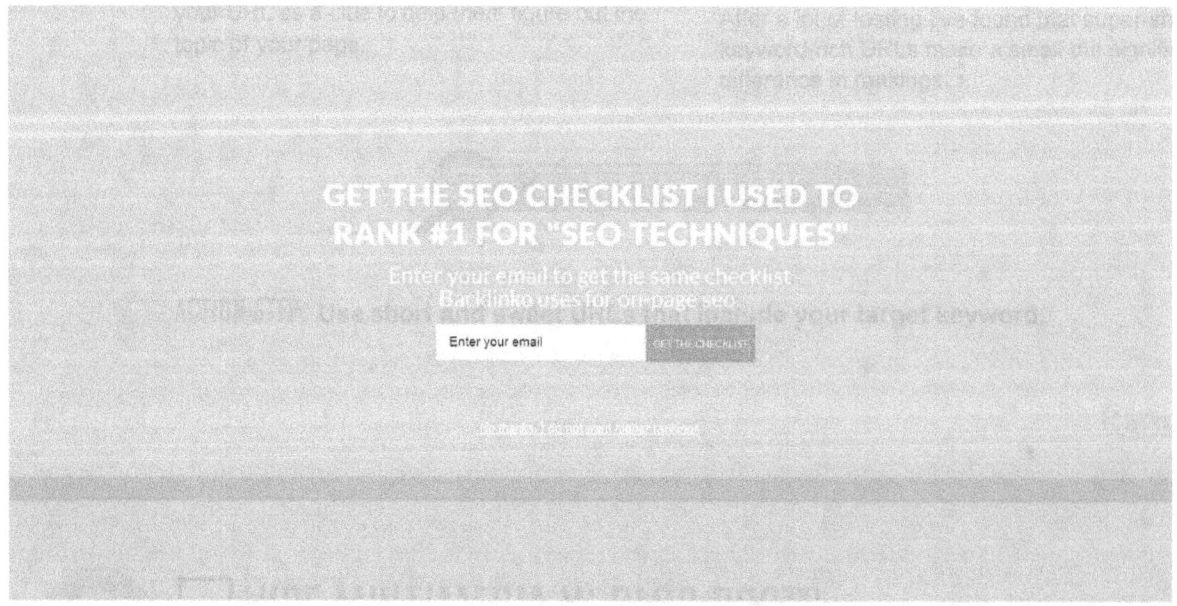

Scroll/Welcome Mats

This type of opt-in form is similar to a screen overlay/takeover in that it consumes the entire page; however, it's different because you can either opt-in or **scroll down** (as opposed to close it)**.**

Scroll/welcome mats give visitors the ability to scroll down which makes the opt-in form a little less obtrusive; they don't have to "hunt" around for a close button … they just have to scroll down.

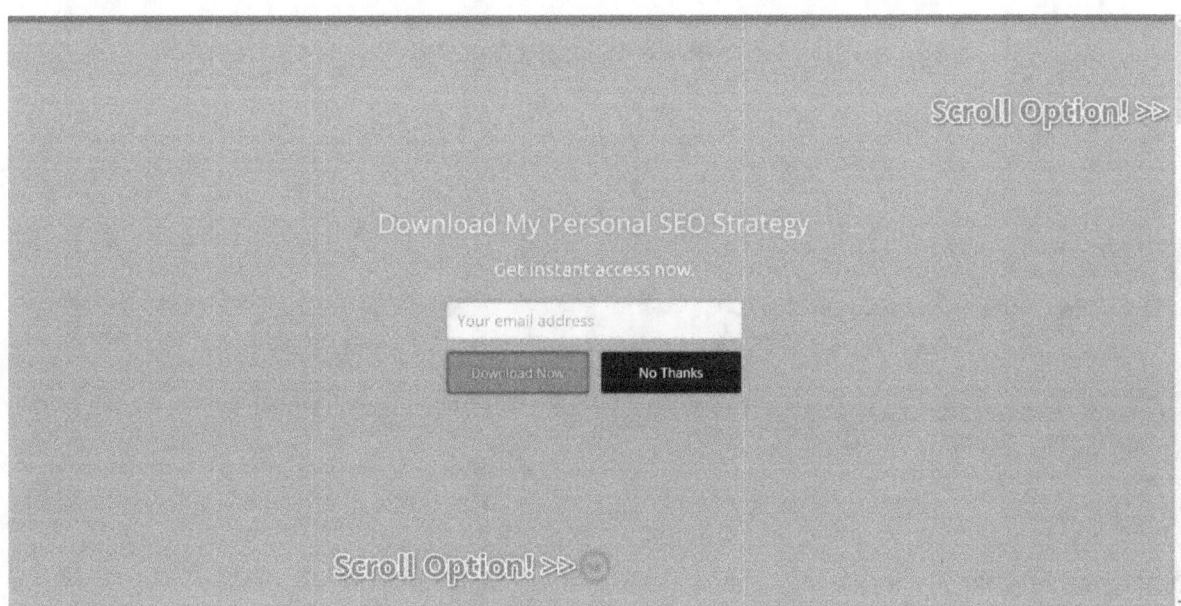

Example From <u>Matthew Woodward</u>

Content Locks

This type of opt-in form is pretty cool because it allows you to protect a piece of content until the individual enters their email address.

This is a great way to offer "<u>content upgrades</u>" to blog posts.

PREMIUM CONTENT

Enter Your Email Below to Unlock All Exclusive Content

Enter your name here...

Enter your email address here...

UNLOCK THIS ARTICLE FOR FREE

Powered by OptinMonster

>> Locked Content <<

Example From OptinMonster

Conclusion

Now that you know the tools, triggers, and types of opt-in forms ... what's stopping you from getting started?

ANNEX D: Email Autoresponder Sequence For Gauging Interest

I served in the Army for four years, and the ingredients for success were simple: be in the proper place, at the proper time, and in the proper uniform.

If I did those three things (plus my job of course) ... I would stand out from my peers. Believe it or not - most people can't do those three simple things.

Anyway, to bring this around to marketing, here's a quote by Jim Yu, CEO BrightEdge:

"The key is to present the right content to the right users at the time they need it in an engaging manner."

Same freakin' concept as my Army days: right content, right users, and at the right time.

Three simple ingredients to standing out from the crowd and being successful.

And, you guessed it - most people and businesses can't do those three simple things.

You'll be able to after reading this article!

Where Does This Email Autoresponder Sequence Go?

The overall concept for this autoresponder sequence is to send a variety of content to our list in an attempt to figure out what each individual is interested in.

Everyone on our list is different. Some are young, some are old, some are single, some are married, some are employees, some are employers, some want to learn and do, while others want you to do it for them.

If you offer a variety of products and services, your list is going to be an even larger hodgepodge; having a system, like I'm about to show you, in place is a requirement.

By gauging interests, we're able to send more relevant and engaging content that ultimately results in more sales.

The left-hand side (Straight Line Sales Funnel / Main Series) of the diagram below shows you where this autoresponder series resides:

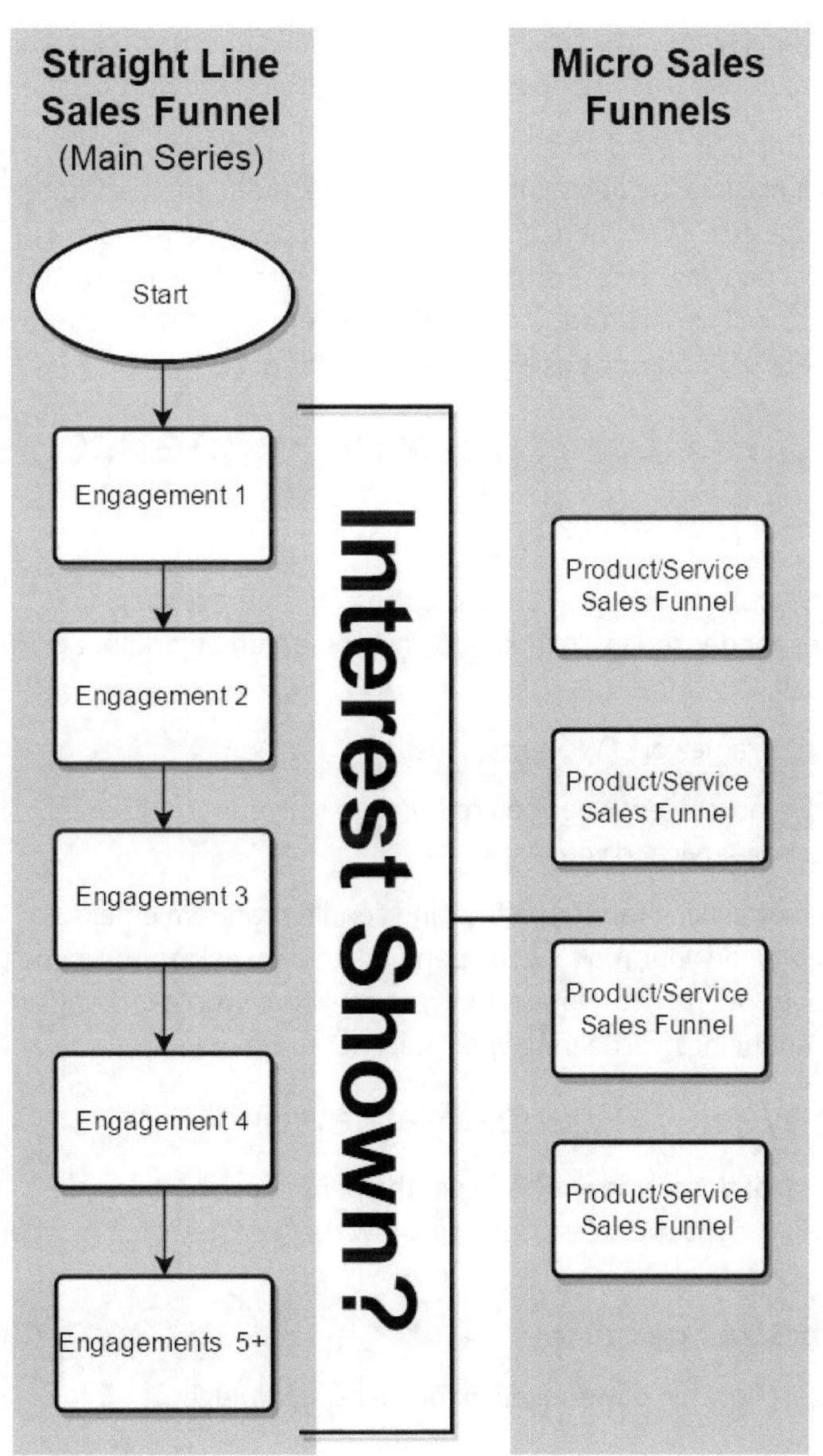

As you see, it goes in a straight line, one email after the other, while simultaneously tracking how individuals interact with particular emails.

For example, if I send an email on the topic of Facebook ads, and the individual clicks the link to the article, I can assume they're interested in Facebook ads. From there, I can pause the "Straight Line Sales Funnel" (interest gauging series), and automatically enter the subscriber into a Micro Sales Funnel (Product/Service Sales Funnel) where I go into more detail about Facebook ads and make an offer or two.

Email Autoresponder Sequence: Weekly "Pushes"

While there are many ways to structure your interest gauging autoresponder series, I'm going to give you a framework that works very well.

I call this framework "Weekly 'Pushes'".

Why? Because every week you're trying to sell (push) a different product or service to your list.

Instead of making random offers and sending random emails depending on your mood, you spend an entire week on the same topic. This gives people more opportunity to see what you're offering and act, while not being overbearing and "burning" them out.

The Weekly "Pushes Framework

The goal of this framework is to get the person on the sales page. If the individual views the sales page, we know they're interested in what we have to offer.

Step 1: Pick a widget to sell.

Step 2: Follow the pattern below for that single widget.

- **Pattern**: 3 and 2 (M, T, W, F, S)

Send 4 to 5 emails on the same topic, for the same widget, during each "push". In general, it's good to break up these emails to give people a little time to react, rather than bombarding them every day. For this reason, I recommend sending 3 daily emails, take a day off, send 2 more daily emails, take a day off, and then repeat with a new "push".

- **Email 1**: Fun/personal story
  - ○ Relate to widget
  - ○ PS goes to sales page

People connect with stories. People enjoy stories. We want people to both connect with us and enjoy hearing from us, which is why we must share a story! Now, it doesn't necessarily have to be a personal story; you can share a success story from a client or customer or even a well known individual, like a celebrity, just shared in a different light.

At the end of the story, close out (soft sell) with a simple PS line that takes them to the sales page where they can learn more, if they wish.

- **Email 2**: Promotion of widget
  - ○ Use a marketing formula: Problem-Agitate-Solve, Feature-Benefits-Advantages, Before-After-Bridge
  - ○ CTA goes directly to the sales page - "Click Here To Buy"

While stories are great and help us connect, sometimes a good old fashioned sales letter converts best ... especially when they have the story from the previous email rolling around in their head! In this 2nd email, pitch your widget. You can use a marketing formula to help structure your message or do whatever you think is best.

The call-to-action should be straight forward and to the point with no mystery behind it, "If you're interested in this widget, click here". (How much more "interest gauging" can you get?! If the person clicks that link, we know they're interested in our offer and they'll enter one of our Micro Sales Funnels.)

- **Emails 3-4:** Content on topic of widget
    - Link to a blog post that's entertaining and/or educational
    - Include CTAs in both the PS line of the email and within the article itself which go to your widget's sales page

After sharing a story and a "hard" pitch, it's time to ease back a little bit and just share some more information with them. Send links to articles, videos, and other resources they'll find helpful, interesting, and entertaining on the same topic as the widget you're trying to sell.

Include links to your widget's sales page in your email PS line and throughout the particular article so they can easily navigate to the sales page, if they're interested in learning more.

- **Email 5:** Content OR Promotion (discount)

Email 5 is optional. If the individual hasn't visited your sales page after 4 emails on the same topic for the same widget ... they may simply not be interested in that offer. So, use some discretion here. If you feel like this 5th email is "too much", don't use it.

If you do use Email 5, you can send another piece of content like emails 3 & 4 OR you can make a last-ditch effort to sell your widget by sending another "hard" sales email and/or by offering a discount.

That is the Weekly "Pushes" framework! Rinse and repeat with a new product the following week!

Getting Content To Send

The Weekly "Pushes" framework requires you to send a fair amount of content, sometimes 3 pieces a week.

This can be a lot, especially for a small business or a new business that hasn't started producing copious amounts of content.

It's OK, there's a way you can share other people's content and *STILL* bring people back to your site.

You can do this by using a tool that adds a bar, bubble, slide-in, popup, etc. to any link you recommend.

There are a handful of tools that allow you to do this, but my favorite is snip.ly.

And, here's an example: http://snip.ly/ld6tx.

They teach you how to use the tool on their site. It's certainly handy and can make up those content "gaps" until you get your own stuff produced!

Conclusion

The way to stand out to your subscribers, leads, and customers is simple...

"The key is to present the right content to the right users at the time they need it in an engaging manner." - Jim Yu, CEO BrightEdge

By using frameworks like the Weekly "Pushes" outlined above, figuring out what people are interested in becomes a piece of cake that can be automated!

ANNEX E: The Amazon Seller's Sales Funnel (Physical Products)

Note: This is a copy of a blog post and is best read as a blog post because it contains several links and a video. If possible, I recommend reading the post on the website as opposed to the book because it will give you a better experience. Here's the link: https://crazyeyemarketing.com/blog/the-amazon-sellers-sales-funnel-clickfunnels/

Selling on Amazon has some MASSIVE benefits ...

- They *give* you traffic

- High conversion rates

- They handle the logistics

But, it has some MASSIVE downsides as well ...

- You don't "own" your customers

- Insane competition

- And, what if they ban you? You're screwed.

Of course, you already know this - these are the reasons you're here, reading this article.

What you've probably done thus far is setup a half-hearted ecommerce store on Shopify "in case" Amazon changes something that disrupts your business.

While your intentions are good, really ... ask yourself ... *"How screwed would I be if Amazon shut me down today?"*

If your answer is anything other than, "I wouldn't even notice it" - you're in the right place!

I'm about to give you a **FREE Sales Funnel** with the full-blown strategy, specifically designed for people like you!

- Here's where you can get your free sales funnel: https://crazyeyemarketing.com/dms/funnels

An Ecommerce Store vs A Sales Funnel

An ecommerce store probably sounds like the right solution to you.

You sell on Amazon which is an ecommerce store, so it seems to make sense that if you make something similar, it should work.

I'm here to tell you, **you're wrong.**

Try it, you'll see.

Running an ecommerce store is hard.

Beyond the technical aspects of building it, automating it, and maintaining it *(that's actually the easy part)* ...

The BIGGEST challenge you're going to have is to CONVINCE someone to buy off your store when there's Amazon.

You will have to build trust.

Building trust takes time and/or money.

You'll probably have to ...

- write great, compelling, trust building copy

- develop a social media presence

- start a blog

- post videos on YouTube

- run paid ads

- handle customer inquiries

- and manage it all

Building trust is hard when you're competing against Amazon.

They already have the trust and you inherit it when you sell on their platform.

But, if you're off their platform ... you're on your own.

You Need To Do Something *Different*

While an ecommerce store may sound like the logical solution, it's not.

It's too hard to compete with Amazon.

You need to do something different.

But, what?

Imagine having a system ...

Imagine having a system where you could put a dollar in and receive at least a dollar in return.

How many dollars would you put into it?

That's the sole purpose of a sales funnel - you put money in, it spits *more* money back out.

Yeah, you're kind of doing it on Amazon already ... it's generating more money than you're putting into it.

But, try running a Facebook ad to your ecommerce store ... let me know how that works out for ya.

Unless you really know what you're doing and have your ducks in a row, I'd be willing to bet big money you will not even break even on paid traffic to your ecommerce store.

It's the nature of the beast.

You need a sales funnel

A Sales Funnel is your answer to the ecommerce store "problem".

With a few working funnels you won't have to worry about Amazon anymore.

The good news is, you already have the products. You already know who your customers are. You already know what sells. You can even use Amazon's Fulfillment Centers.

You already have everything you need. Now, you just need to "funnel-ize" it!

The Amazon Seller's Sales Funnel

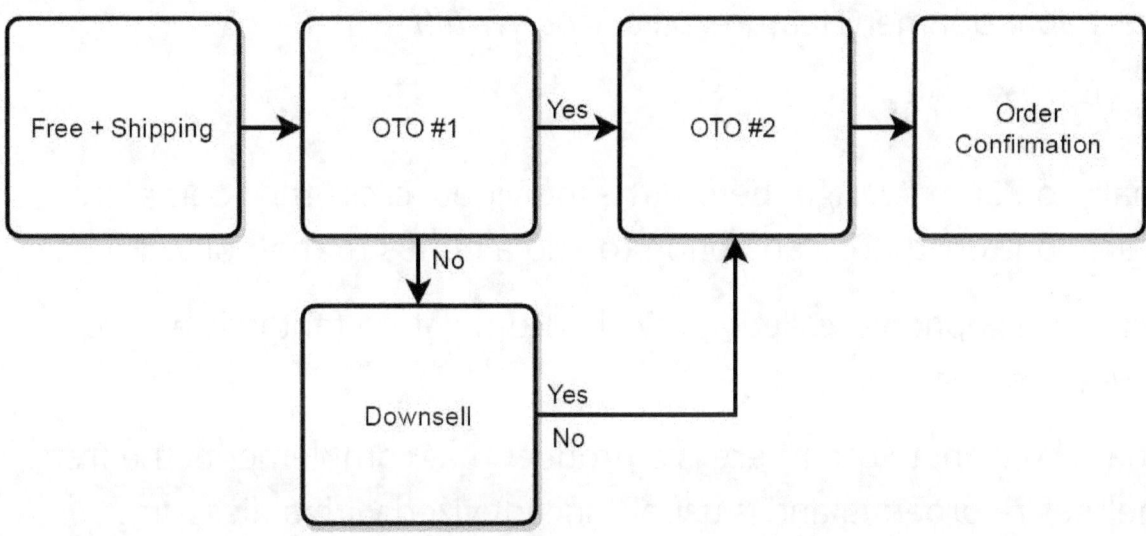

Free + Shipping [**see page**: https://cemllc.clickfunnels.com/p/10367249]

Grow Your List With Buyers

The first page in this sales funnel is a Free + Shipping offer.

What does that mean? It means you give something away for free, all they have to do is pay shipping & handling!

This is a great way to get BUYERS on your list - people that have proven they'll spend money with you.

There's no reason you can't create a Free + Shipping offer for your business. There must be a product you can acquire for under $2 that your audience will love (if you don't have one already).

Tip: incorporate the cost of the product in the shipping & handling price.

Cart Abandonment

Another cool feature of the Free + Shipping page is the 2-step form.

If someone inputs their contact info and goes to Step #2 (billing info), but doesn't pay, you will still capture their contact information. You can then re-engage them via email, phone, and/or snail mail. Think of it like a cart abandonment feature. *(Really powerful!)*

Order Bumps

Finally, on Step #2, right before the individual clicks the "Complete Order" button, there's an option to add a bonus to their order.

This bonus option is called an "Order Bump; it's a fantastic way to increase order size.

What you want to offer here is a product that complements the free one they're ordering and is usually incentivized with a discount.

For example, with my Crazy Mug, I could include some Crazy Coffee Beans for 30% off.

Another option that works really well is to ask if the individual would like to double or even triple their order!

I'm about to run some numbers; if you hate numbers - skip to the next section.

Let's say my Crazy Mug costs me $1.50 to get in the Amazon warehouse. Amazon charges me $5.95 to ship it. However, to ship a second one, they only charge $1.20. So, to give away 2 mugs, it costs me $10.15 ($3 for 2 mugs + shipping & handling). If I charge $5.99 shipping & handling per mug, that brings in $11.98 and I'm able to net $1.83. Yes, not much in this particular example; however, what if my product cost was closer to $0.50? What if people were tripling their orders? There are lots of things to try!

OTO #1 (One-Time-Offer) [see page:
https://cemllc.clickfunnels.com/p/10367250]

Obviously, you'll go out of business if you only give away free stuff.

You're going to have to make money somewhere in this funnel, and the first place to really make it is with OTO #1!

OTO stands for One-Time-Offer and it's essentially a special offer presented to an individual, only one time, which is *right now!* If they don't act now, they miss out on this exclusive offer forever. This added element of scarcity increases conversions.

Typically, OTO #1 should be around $50; however, depending on your market, it could be more. It's typically less than OTO #2. *(This is just what's "typical" - heck, try selling some really expensive stuff in OTO #1 and see what happens!)*

While there are several strategies and tactics for OTOs - the main objective of your OTO in this sales funnel is to **sell something that has an incredibly high margin**. This will allow you to recoup ad spend and turn a profit.

Hopefully you already have some incredibly high margin products in your inventory that even when paired with an irresistible discount, you're still able to reap a nice profit.

However, what if you don't have an incredibly high margin product to offer? Here are some ideas that work well:

- **Create a bundle** - combine a few products so the OTO, as a whole, has a higher value

- **Add digital assets** - courses, training, documents, membership

  - Video Training: <u>How to build a membership portal in ClickFunnels</u> (https://www.youtube.com/watch?v=4IiRsZ_zFNw)

- **Introduce continuity** *(recurring)* - membership, community

- **Add a subscription** *(recurring)* - consumable products typically need to be replaced, can you offer a subscription service?

The Video

The video included in the funnel is just a placeholder. You need to shoot your own video or you can make a text based offer if you'd rather; however, video typically converts better.

The video should only be 3-5 minutes in length and hit on a few key points:

- Tell them the free product they just grabbed is freakin' awesome and will be on its way to them shortly. Reiterate a key benefit or two.

- Introduce the OTO as a special offer that's going to make that free product even better.
  - Also, hit on the fact that this offer is not for everyone. It's only for individuals that have grabbed the free product.
- Tell them what the OTO is and how it will benefit them.
- Tell them to click the "orange" button below to accept the offer.
- If you offer a guarantee, mention it.
- Share a review or two. Or at least snippets with the key points.
- Tell them to again click the "orange" button below to accept the offer.

If you hit on all of those points, you'll easily fill the 3-5 minutes!

What An OTO Is Not

An OTO should not be an upgrade of the free product they just grabbed.

For example, if I'm giving away coffee mugs, my OTO should not be a really expensive coffee mug because they already requested a mug … why would they need another one?

Instead, what you offer needs to *complement* what they just purchased, not replace it.

Downsell [see page: https://cemllc.clickfunnels.com/p/10367251]

Unfortunately, not everyone is going to accept your OTO #1, no matter how awesome it is.

For the people that say "no" to OTO #1, offer them a downsell.

There are a few ways to handle this:

1. **Offer a discount on the OTO #1** - Like in the funnel I'm giving away, the downsell is a discount on OTO #1. This option can work incredibly well; however, bear in mind your margins as well as how you want to be perceived. Are you sure you want to "reward" people for saying "no"? However, if it's more of a "churn and burn" play as opposed to brand building - this option may work well for you.

2. **Add a bonus** - Add another product to OTO #1, physical or digital to sweeten the deal. Note: similar to providing a discount, this option may inadvertently "train" people to say "no" so they can see what bonuses they'll receive.

3. **Break up OTO #1** - If your OTO #1 is a bundle, break it up and allow people to purchase pieces of it individually. This works well because your customer may not want all of the items included in the bundle; however, if offered a discount on one of the products, they'll take it.

4. **Offer a payment plan** - Instead of one payment of $47, can you make it 2 payments of $23.50? This may entice your customer to make the purchase, but make sure you're not going to lose money if they only pay one payment. (Tip: include a "just charge me the onetime payment of $47" option in addition to the payment plan option.).

5. **"Are you sure?"** - Offer the exact same OTO #1 again. Reiterate the fact that it *really* is a one-time offer and they won't see it again.

OTO #2 [see page: https://cemllc.clickfunnels.com/p/10367252]

Whether or not your new customer purchases OTO #1 or the Downsell, they are presented with OTO #2.

OTO #2 is usually one of three things:

1. **A higher-end, more expensive product** - While OTO #1 is typically cheaper at around $50, and more "reasonable" to purchase, OTO #2 is typically one of your more expensive products. One where you're celebrating if it sells (as long as it's in line with everything else you're selling in your funnel).

2. **Another product that complements the Free + Shipping product** - If you don't have any expensive products to offer, that's OK. You can still recommend another complementary product that helps your customer while simultaneously increasing order size.

3. **A continuity offer (if not included with OTO #1)** - A membership or subscription that provides recurring revenue is the holy grail. It provides consistency and predictability to your business. If you can fit one in somewhere, do it.

Like OTO #1, you want to use a 3-5 minute video to sell it. You can follow a similar script as the one outlined above.

Order Confirmation [see page: https://cemllc.clickfunnels.com/p/10370219]

The Order Confirmation page is simply that, a page that confirms the individual's order.

It simply thanks them for their order, breaks it down for them, and tells them how to get in touch, what to expect, and what to do next.

Offer Wall

An Offer Wall is what it sounds like, a wall of offers. Essentially, you'll display 3-6 products with links to them and possibly some exclusive discounts. If your new customer wants to buy more from you, they know where to look!

I didn't include one of these with the sales funnel I'm giving away. However, it's relatively simple to add and something you may want to consider doing!

ClickFunnels to Amazon FBA

Since you're already selling on Amazon, I'm sure you're taking advantage of their fulfillment centers.

This is the best way I know how to connect ClickFunnels to Amazon FBA: https://www.youtube.com/watch?v=_q11KRfTqSg&lc

Take Action!

Now is the time for you to make a decision.

Are you going to stay dependent on Amazon while running a half-hearted ecommerce store *or* are you going to take control, build a few funnels, and dominate?!

Grab your free "Physical Products" Funnel here: https://crazyeyemarketing.com/dms/funnels

ANNEX F: A Sales Funnel For Selling Digital Products

Note: *This is a copy of a blog post and is best read as a blog post because it contains several links and a video. If possible, I recommend reading the post on the website as opposed to the book because it will give you a better experience. Here's the link:*
https://crazyeyemarketing.com/blog/a-sales-funnel-for-selling-digital-products-clickfunnels/

Imagine owning a machine that prints money.

Every time you put in $1, you get that $1 *plus* back.

Whether it's spitting out $1.01 or $6, you'd run that machine all day.

And, that's the dream, right?

To have a reliable system that generates a consistent ROI?

The problem is, it's not easy to do.

Plus, you're constantly pushed in a million different directions.

Should you ...

- Start a blog?

- Focus on social media?

- Build backlinks?

- Setup email automation?

- Guest blog?

- Start a podcast?

- Run Facebook Ads?

- Run Adwords?

- Make YouTube videos?

- And the list continues ...

Unfortunately, **these activities aren't the machine**; however, they're what most small businesses and entrepreneurs focus on.

Instead, these activities are the **machine's fuel.**

The point?

You need a machine before you need the fuel.

And, I want to give you a machine _**for FREE!**_

- **https://crazyeyemarketing.com/dms/funnels**

The Digital Product(s) Sales Funnel (The Machine)

The sales funnel I'm about to describe is perfect for businesses that sell digital goods like courses, ebooks, resources, memberships, etc.

Here's an overview of the sales funnel:

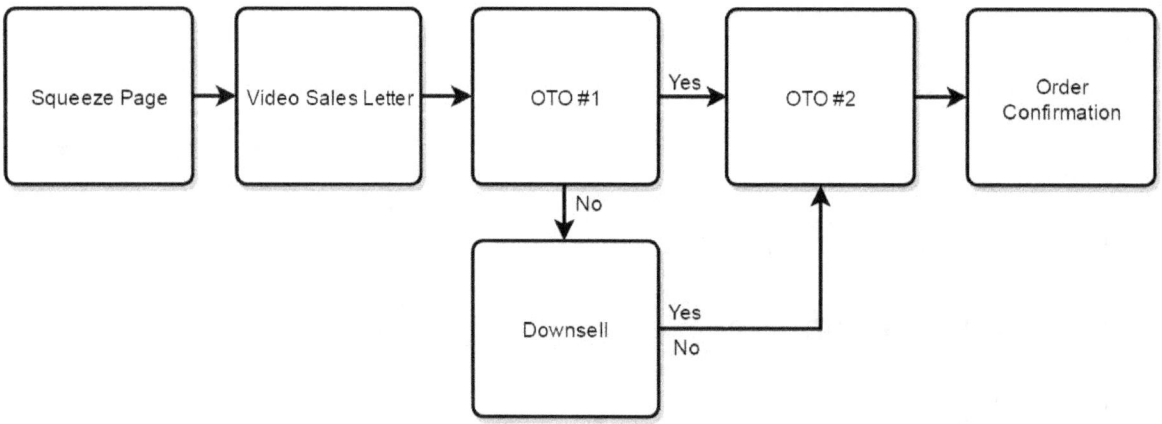

Squeeze Page [see page: https://cemllc.clickfunnels.com/p/10538653]

The first page in this sales funnel is what's called a Squeeze Page.

Its name is derived from the fact it "squeezes" the contact information out of the visitor.

This is typically accomplished by offering an incentive called a Lead Magnet.

Once you have the individual's contact information, you're able to engage with them to help move them through the funnel.

The Squeeze Page included with this funnel is my **top converting squeeze page of all time**.

Yes, it's plain, but I constantly test it against prettier pages and it always wins.

Video Sales Letter (VSL) [see page: https://cemllc.clickfunnels.com/p/10538654]

The Video Sales Letter (VSL) is exactly like it sounds ... a video that acts as a sales letter.

Instead of writing a long form sales page that takes hours and possibly days, you can shoot a 3-6 minute video in less than an hour.

Customers typically prefer video over the long sales pages. Or, you can always kill two birds with one stone and include a video plus a little write-up that outlines what you talk about in the video.

Win-win, you do less time-consuming work and customers like it more!

What should you say in your VSL? I recommend starting with Jim Edwards' "How To Write Great Video Sales Letter Script" Formula (http://thejimedwardsmethod.com/the-great-video-sales-letter-script-formula/).

What Should You Sell?

There are several schools of thought here and I'll explain a couple, but it's by no means all inclusive.

Tripwire / Self-Liquidating Offer (SLO)

A Tripwire or Self-Liquidating Offer is a cheap product (usually under $10) that's so amazing people can't *NOT* buy it.

The idea behind it is to get the individual to open their wallet, qualify themselves as a buyer, and once you make this initial sale - the next should be easier.

Tripwires and SLOs can help you recoup ad spend.

However, they may attract low quality leads that are "bargain hunters" who will never buy any OTOs or upsells.

Your Core Product (Reversed Value Ladder)

Instead of going the whole Tripwire/SLO route, why not try and sell what you *actually* want to sell?

If they don't take your offer, you can then recommend lower priced versions of it.

Maybe they don't want your full-blown Facebook Ads course for $197, but they'll take your ads cheat sheet & walkthrough for $27, or just the cheat sheet for $7.

There are many ways to structure this portion and the bulk of your time will likely be placed on testing which structure works best for your business, product, and audience.

Timed Price/Button Reveal

If you look at the example page (https://cemllc.clickfunnels.com/p/10538654), you won't see a button or order form until 15 seconds have passed. *(you can adjust this to any amount of time)*

The idea behind this tactic is that you draw the person in, make them *crave* your product, and have them thinking it's going to be *super* expensive. Then, when you mention the price, you also display the "Order Now" button and the corresponding order form.

By the time you show them the price, they're already sold and they buy it right away!

That's the idea at least, but does this tactic work?

Run a split test inside ClickFunnels - one variation with the delay, one without, and see which wins! Different audiences behave differently so the only way to be sure what's best for yours is to test.

OTO #1 (One-Time-Offer) [see page:
https://cemllc.clickfunnels.com/p/10538655]

Hurray! Someone purchased your initial offer from the VSL page, and whether it was a Tripwire or your Core Offer ... *their wallet is open and they're in buying mode!*

OTO stands for One-Time-Offer and it's essentially a special offer presented to an individual, only one time, which is *right now!* If they don't act now, they miss out on this exclusive offer forever. This added element of scarcity increases conversions.

Typically, OTO #1 is one of two things:

1. **Your Core Offer**, if you offered a Tripwire or SLO. This is the course or resource that you "really" want to sell.

2. **A Continuity Offer**, if you offered your core offer as the initial offer. For example, some type of membership site, community, or additional support that's recurring.

Either way, it should complement what they just purchased.

The Video

The video included in the funnel example is just a placeholder. You need to shoot your own video or you can make a text based offer if you'd rather; however, video typically converts better.

The video should only be 3-5 minutes in length and hit on a few key points:

- Tell them the Tripwire/SLO or Core Offer they just grabbed is awesome and they'll have instant access to it in just a minute. Reiterate a key benefit or two.

- Introduce the OTO as a special offer that's going to make what they just purchased even better.

    o Also, hit on the fact that this offer is not for everyone. It's only for individuals that have grabbed the Initial Offer.

- Tell them what the OTO is and how it will benefit them.

- Tell them to click the "orange" button below to accept the offer.

- If you offer a guarantee, mention it.

- Share a review/testimonial or two. Or at least snippets with the key points.

- Tell them to again click the "orange" button below to accept the offer.

If you hit on all of those points, you'll easily fill the 3-5 minutes!

Downsell [see page: https://cemllc.clickfunnels.com/p/10538657]

Sadly, not everyone is going to accept your OTO #1, no matter how awesome it is.

For the people that say "no" to OTO #1, offer them a downsell.

If OTO #1 was ...

... your Core Offer, you can:

- Offer a payment plan. Instead of $197 today, they can join for 3 monthly payments of $67.

- Add a bonus. ie. Additional training, a complementary course, coaching, etc.

- Offer a straight-up discount.

... a Continuity Offer, you can:

- Offer them to join the first month for only $1. (or as low as is practical)

OTO #2 [see page: https://cemllc.clickfunnels.com/p/10538658]

Whether or not your new customer purchases OTO #1 or the Downsell, they are presented with OTO #2.

OTO #2 is usually one of three things:

1. **A Profit Maximizer** - A really expensive course, membership, or coaching package. We're looking at the $1,000 dollar range.

2. **Another complementary course or resource** - If you don't have a Profit Maximizer to offer, maybe you can offer another product/resource that complements the initial offer. Even if it's cheaper than OTO #1, that's OK. You can still increase cart order size!

3. **A Continuity Offer** *(if not already offered)* - If you didn't make a continuity offer in OTO #1, OTO #2 may be a great place to present one.

Like OTO #1, you probably want to use a 3-5 minute video to sell it. You can follow a similar script as the one outlined above.

Order Confirmation [see page:

https://cemllc.clickfunnels.com/p/10538659]

The Order Confirmation page is simply that, a page that confirms the individual's order.

It simply thanks them for their order, breaks it down for them, and tells them how to get in touch, what to expect, and what to do next.

Offer Wall

An Offer Wall is what it sounds like, a wall of offers. Essentially, you'll display 3-6 more products and/or services with links to them and possibly some exclusive discounts. If your new customer wants to buy more from you, they know where to look!

I didn't include one of these with the sales funnel I'm giving away. However, it's relatively simple to add and something you may want to consider doing!

Take Action!

Now is the time for you to make a decision.

Are you going to continue to focus on "the fuel" *or* are you going to build the machine?!

Grab your free "Digital Products" Funnel here:
https://crazyeyemarketing.com/dms/funnels

ANNEX G: The Coaching/Consulting "Book" Sales Funnel

Note: This is a copy of a blog post and is best read as a blog post because it contains several links and a video. If possible, I recommend reading the post on the website as opposed to the book because it will give you a better experience. Here's the link: https://crazyeyemarketing.com/blog/the-coaching-consulting-book-sales-funnel-clickfunnels/

Books are the new business card.

Having a book helps you establish your expertise, makes you appear credible, sets you apart from your competition, and can bring you new business *(if used properly)*.

Thanks to self-publishing services, anyone can write a book and have it professionally printed within weeks.

For this reason, many coaches, consultants, service providers, and educators have started using books in their efforts to bring in new business.

If you have, or are planning to have, your own book ... I've got a free sales funnel for you to bring in new business!

- **https://crazyeyemarketing.com/dms/funnels**

Why Is A Book A Great Front-End Offer?

Beyond the whole "business card" concept, a book makes a great front-end offer because it's usually a low barrier to entry (less than $10), qualifies leads, educates them on what you do, and **it's physical**.

Physical products carry more weight (both literally and figuratively) than digital products.

People can actually hold it, feel it, touch it, smell it ... and, it takes up space on their desk, coffee table, toilet, etc.

A piece of you will be with them, in their house/office, serving as a constant reminder that you're the guy/gal they want to do business with!

Plus, since it's a physical product, you have to ship it to them. This is a great excuse to get them to give you all of their "real" contact information which allows you to add them to various lists (retargeting, email, text, direct mail, etc.) for continued marketing.

If you're a coach, consultant, service provider, or educator and you're wondering what you should offer to get people in the door, a book is a great place to start.

The Coaching/Consulting "Book" Sales Funnel

Here is an overview of the sales funnel:

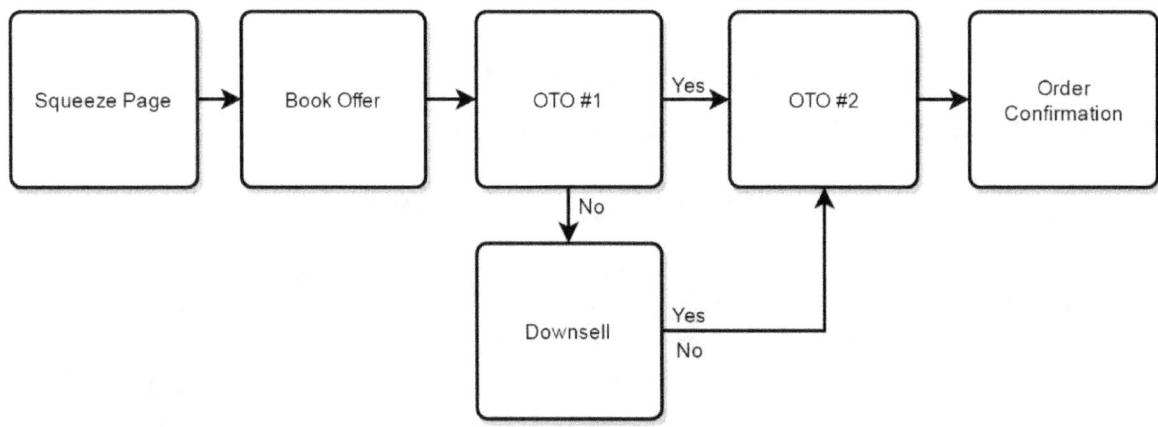

Squeeze Page [see page: https://cemllc.clickfunnels.com/p/10379043]

The first page in this sales funnel is what's called a Squeeze Page.

It's name is derived from the fact it "squeezes" the contact information out of the visitor.

This is typically accomplished by offering an incentive called a Lead Magnet.

Once you have the individual's contact information, you're able to engage with them to help move them through the funnel.

The Squeeze Page included with this funnel is my **top converting squeeze page of all time**.

Yes, it's plain, but I constantly test it against prettier pages and it always wins.

Give Away A Part Of The Book ...

For your Lead Magnet, you will likely want to give away part of the book because this can help setup the sale of the book itself.

Which part?

A Chapter

If it makes sense to give away a chapter - you can do that, but make sure it's a great one and draws them into the rest of the book!

Unfortunately, giving out a chapter can hinder conversions because people will figure they'll read the free chapter first, then go buy the book. The problem here is they'll never read the free chapter and never buy your book. So, that's something to be mindful of and you may want to test your free chapter against another Lead Magnet.

A Chart/Graph/Table/Story

If applicable, yank out the sexiest chart/graph/table/story you have in your book, shoot a short 3-5 minute explainer video about it, and give that away.

This way, your lead will get a piece of content that's easily consumable and can decide then and there to go and buy your book.

Book Offer [see page: https://cemllc.clickfunnels.com/p/10318040]

This is the sales page for your book.

It's setup as a Free + Shipping offer. This means, the individual gets a free book - all they have to do is cover the shipping costs.

Tip: Include the cost of the book in the price of shipping, this way you're breaking even on the book.

The page itself is pretty self-explanatory:

- Include a picture/video of the book

- Add some reviews and testimonials, whether video or text

- Tell them what they'll learn in the book

- Include a note/bio from the author and/or a little pitch on why you're giving it away for free

Whether you decide to present it as a Free + Shipping offer or not, do your best to keep the total cost under $10.

The Order Bump

On step two of the order form, there's the option for an order bump.

An order bump gives the visitor a chance to add something to their order before they submit their payment information. *(and a chance for you to sell something!)*

Some great order bumps for books are:

- An audio version

- Complementary training/course

- Coaching call

- Video exclusive

These bumps typically convert best between $27 and $37.

OTO #1 (One-Time-Offer) [see page: https://cemllc.clickfunnels.com/p/10318264]

Yay! Someone purchased your book! Their wallet is now open and they're in buying mode!

OTO stands for One-Time-Offer and it's essentially a special offer presented to an individual, only one time, which is *right now!* If they don't act now, they miss out on this exclusive offer forever. This added element of scarcity increases conversions.

Typically, OTO #1 is your core offer.

This can be the digital course you really want to sell, or one that at least complements the book they just purchased.

OTO #1 could also be a coaching plan or service you offer.

Whatever it is, it's typically the reason you wrote the book in the first place - to sell this particular product/service.

The Video

The video included in the funnel example is just a placeholder. You need to shoot your own video or you can make a text based offer if you'd rather; however, video typically converts better.

The video should only be 3-5 minutes in length and hit on a few key points:

- Tell them the book they just grabbed is awesome and you'll ship it to them within 24 hours. Reiterate a key benefit or two.

- Introduce the OTO as a special offer that's going to make what they just purchased even better.

  - Also, hit on the fact that this offer is not for everyone. It's only for individuals that have grabbed the Initial Offer.

- Tell them what the OTO is and how it will benefit them.

- Tell them to click the "orange" button below to accept the offer.

- If you offer a guarantee, mention it.

- Share a review/testimonial or two. Or at least snippets with the key points.

- Tell them to again click the "orange" button below to accept the offer.

If you hit on all of those points, you'll easily fill the 3-5 minutes!

Downsell [see page: https://cemllc.clickfunnels.com/p/10323022]

Unfortunately, not everyone is going to accept your OTO #1, no matter how awesome it is.

For the people that say "no" to OTO #1, offer them a downsell.

A few downsell ideas include:

- **A payment plan:** Offer them the chance to join your course or acquire your services for a few, monthly, installment payments.

- **A bonus:** Offer an additional resource, training, coaching call, or service to motivate them to take you up on your offer

- **A discount:** Offer a straight up discount on OTO #1.

- **A modified OTO #1:** Offer a "stripped down" or modified version of OTO #1. For example, instead of getting all the video tutorials, they'll only get the PDF documents.

- **An entirely different offer:** Offer something else, but along the same topic. For example, OTO #1 is about advertising on Facebook, and the downsell is about advertising on Google Adwords. Both offers deal with traffic, but they're different.

OTO #2 [see page: https://cemllc.clickfunnels.com/p/10323112]

Whether or not your new customer purchases OTO #1 or the Downsell, they are presented with OTO #2.

OTO #2 is usually one of three things:

1. **A Profit Maximizer** - A really expensive course, membership, service, or coaching package. We're looking at the $1,000 range.

2. **Another complementary course or resource** - If you don't have a Profit Maximizer to offer, maybe you can offer another product/resource that also complements your book. Even if it's cheaper than OTO #1, that's OK. You can still increase cart order size!

3. **A Continuity Offer** - Some form of recurring membership.

Like OTO #1, you probably want to use a 3-5 minute video to sell it. You can follow a similar script as the one outlined above.

Order Confirmation [see page: https://cemllc.clickfunnels.com/p/10375510]

The Order Confirmation page is simply that, a page that confirms the individual's order.

It simply thanks them for their order, breaks it down for them, and tells them how to get in touch, what to expect, and what to do next.

Offer Wall

An Offer Wall is what it sounds like, a wall of offers. Essentially, you'll display 3-6 more products and/or services with links to them and possibly some exclusive discounts. If your new customer wants to buy more from you, they know where to look!

I didn't include one of these with the sales funnel I'm giving away. However, it's relatively simple to add and something you may want to consider doing!

Take Action!

Now is the time for you to make a decision.

Are you going to use a book to explode your business *or* are you going to keep passing out lame business cards?!

Grab your free "Book" Funnel here: https://crazyeyemarketing.com/dms/funnels